The Back Road Mysteries

"Book Two"

"The Tower"

By

Jimmy Zeigler

Dedication

To my beloved wife, Martha, my first-line proofreader and partner for nearly 58 wonderful years.

This book is for you.

Acknowledgment

Casper Williams, Writers of the US has helped me get this book in shape to be published.

Contents

Dedication i

Acknowledgment ii

About the Author v

Chapter One 1

Chapter Two 6

Chapter Three 9

Chapter Four 12

Chapter Five 16

Chapter Six 19

Chapter Seven 22

Chapter Eight 26

Chapter Nine 33

Chapters Ten 36

Chapter Eleven 45

Chapter Twelve 49

Chapter Thirteen 54

Chapter Fourteen 59

Chapter Fifteen 63

Chapter Sixteen 70

Chapter Seventeen 77

Chapter Eighteen 80

Chapter Nineteen 86

Chapter Twenty 97

Chapter Twenty-One 106

Chapter Twenty-Two 111

Chapter Twenty-Three 120

About the Author

James (Jimmy) F. Zimmerman, a native of New Castle, Virginia, is the author of this novel. He and his wife have shared a special bond since their marriage in 1966. This book marks his eleventh work, following the publication of his earlier novels.

His debut book, Love or Lust, was well-received, and he followed it with The Church, the first installment in his seven-book series, The Back Road Mysteries. The series, set in Craig County, Virginia, continues with *The Tower, The Pond, The Mine, The Old Brick Hotel, The Disappearing Town*, and the recently completed *The Bloody Bucket*. He has also penned three additional manuscripts: One of Five, The Agency, and The Back Steps. The Agency is available on Amazon and is not connected to the Back Road Mysteries series.

James F. Zimmerman is passionate about his writing, and he hopes you will find enjoyment in his latest work.

This story begins where The Back Road Mysteries/The Church left off: This book starts out at Janet and Clifford's wedding. They have to deal with a woman's body hanging from an abandoned Forestry Fire Tower and trying to get Janet pregnant. These two things are just a few of the trials they have in this novel.

Chapter One

This story begins with the wedding of Janet and Cliff in the little town of New Castle, Virginia. The last book ended with an entry that they were married and lived happily ever after. Maybe or maybe not is the question!

Janet is standing in her living room, putting her veil on. She and her mother had gotten the form-fitting wedding dress on her without too much effort. It was a snug fit, but she felt she looked nice in it, and Clifford would definitely take notice when she walked down the aisle of the church. Her dad came in the door just as she was putting the veil on her head.

Honey girl, you look wonderful; if Cliff doesn't grab you when you go down that aisle, some man will for sure. She smiled at him and replied, yes, Dad, that is the plan; I will not leave that church without a husband on my arm. They both laughed; each knew that the only man on her arm would be her Cliff.

Dad, can you reach up on the top of my head and make sure this veil is fastened? I would hate being halfway down the aisle and it falling off behind me or maybe falling down the front and me stepping on it and falling. Mr. Moore walked behind her, gave it a little pull, and proclaimed that it was secure and for her not to worry.

Dad, I love you and will miss you, but Cliff will calm me down once we are married. Her father gave out a big chuckle at that, daughter, your mother and I have not been able to calm you down, no matter how hard we tried. Do you really think one little man will be able to? Smiling, she replied, well, he can try, can't he? With that, her Dad went on into the kitchen to grab one last cup of black coffee; he wished he could have a little stronger drink to calm him down. He was about to lose his only little girl to another man, and she would never be his girl anymore. He wiped back a little tear from his eye when he thought this to himself.

Drinking his coffee, he went up the back stairs to get ready to escort his daughter down the aisle and hand her off to Cliff. He only hoped he did not cry walking her down the aisle.

When he reached the bedroom, his wife was just finishing fixing her hair. My sweet, I don't know which of my women is the prettiest today, you or our young daughter. He walked over to her as she arose from the make-up table chair, put his arms around her, and gave her a light kiss so as not to mess up her makeup. That would have been a cardinal sin on a day like today. She lightly kissed him back in appreciation of the affection he had just shown her.

They both finished dressing and went down the stairs. As they entered the living room, there stood Janet in her wedding dress, ready to go to the church. Her mother's eyes grew moist, but she refused to cry and mess up her makeup. Her father helped her get in their car and headed down the mountain to New Castle to the Church. They could see Clifford's car was already in the parking lot as they pulled in.

Janet went directly to the back of the Church and into the room that all the brides used to hold up in until it was time to walk down the aisle or off the plank, depending on how you felt that day. Her mother checked on things in the large family center to make sure the food for the reception was there. Their friend Joan was in charge, and she had seen to everything. Mrs. Moore went in to join her daughter to help keep her calm, cool, and collected. It would only be about an hour until the service would be starting, and she would lose her daughter; she tried to think of it as gaining a son, but she knew better.

When a woman leaves her parents to be joined by her husband, that's it; the really close bond is transferred to the husband, and rightly so. Her father was just hanging around the entrance to the church, waiting for the time for him to give his daughter away, when Clifford walked up the steps and over to him with a big grin on his face.

Good afternoon, Mr. Moore. How are you holding up? I am feeling fine; you are the one who should be anxious! Why is that? Clifford asked. Mr. Moore smiled back and politely replied and said, Cliff, son, you are about to embark down the path of being a husband to a headstrong woman. I know; I am her father and have been trying to tame the shrew for twenty-some-odd years now without any success.

Best wishes and good luck to you my son, you are going to need both. Clifford almost bent double laughing, I know but I love her just the way she is and would not want to change her at all. Thanks for the warning, Dad, can I call you that? Sure, Cliff, he replied:

The minister motioned for them to come to the front of the Church; it was just about time for the service to begin. Cliff went to the front of the Church, and Mr. Moore went to escort his daughter around to the entrance door and down the aisle. The Church was full of family and friends, and the music had begun to be played.

The little flower girl came down the aisle, dropping rose petals on the white runner, and then the best man and maid of honor came down arm in arm, a little different than most weddings. Then, the three bride's maids with an usher on their arm.

Now, the ring bearer was marching down the aisle. He was only four years old, but he had been given good instructions by his Dad on what to do, and he loved Clifford.

The little tyke walked straight down the aisle and stood right beside Clifford and the best man. The Bridal March began, and Clifford's knees started to quiver a little. Oh me, why am I starting to get nervous, Clifford said to himself, shape up and act like a man.

Janet was almost to him now, and she looked beautiful to Cliff. Her father placed her hand in Cliff's after lifting her veil and giving her one last kiss on the cheek. Cliff took her hand, and other than saying, I do, he could not have told you anything that had happened after he took her hand.

Clifford finally came to his senses while on the dance floor with his new bride. Janet, I am sorry if I seemed distracted for a while. It was like I was in a dream during the wedding, and now I am just waking up. He gave her a soft kiss on her lips, and she returned the kiss. The food that was catered for the reception was delicious.

The small country restaurant chef knew how to cook. They had baked apples, pork tenderloin that melted in your mouth, fried country ham, sweet potatoes with marsh-mellow topping, along with two or three kinds of cold salads and, of course, green beans.

The Wedding Cake was a four-tier with different flavors in each layer with that flavor of icing between that layer and the next, and the whole cake was covered on the outside with ten-minute icing, that was to die for.

The band was a local group that played everything and had a guy who could belt out a melody as well as any well-known singer. The reception lasted until about ten o'clock before the bride and groom were able to slip away.

Chapter Two

The couple went to Clifford's house and changed into their traveling clothes. Their flight to Raleigh, North Carolina, departed Roanoke at midnight and landed in North Carolina at two o'clock. They had a room near the airport for their Honeymoon Night already reserved for them. By the time they had arrived there, it was almost three a.m., and both of them were tired from the long wedding day.

They pulled the sheets back and let their clothes just fall on the floor and got in naked as Blue Jays, as the old saying goes. I personally don't know what a naked Blue Jay looks like. They wrapped around one another and got all snuggled up and the next thing either knew was Janet waking up to Clifford's voice.

Darling, are you going to get up anytime today? She opened her eyes, and Cliff was propped up on one arm, staring down at her with a smile on his face. She could see that the sheet that was covering his manhood was standing up, so she knew they were about to get together for the first time as man and wife. He turned over to her and slid his slim body on top of hers, and that was all it took; she responded to him, and he knew the love she felt for him by the way she reacted.

Cliff, have we got everything out of the room now? I wouldn't want to have to drive back to get something. I have it all, hon he said; just get in the car, and we can get on to the Outer Banks. They got into the rental car and started on their way. It was to be a three-hour trip to OBX, and when they pulled into the realty company that Cliff had rented the house from, the time reflected three hours. They were walking into the small older house that was in the middle of Kill Devil Hills beach and set right on the beach.

All you had to do was go out the back door and down three steps, and you were on the beach. Janet went through the two-bedroom cottage looking at all of the things that the owners over the years had brought and left. She could see things that told her what the owner must be like. There was nothing trashy in the house, and most everything in it had to be at least fifty years old.

The dishes in the kitchen were white Fire King with gold rings and flowers. The silverware was silver-plated dinnerware and beautiful stemmed goblets to drink out of. The furniture was from another era in time; it was made of maple wood with cushions on the seat and back. You could tell they had been recovered but were still in good shape and comfortable. The kitchen had an old oak table and chairs, but they were in pristine shape.

The people had refrained from putting anything personal on the walls, but they did have beautiful paintings hanging in all the rooms. They had asked about the cottage and were told that it had been built during the 1930s and had been owned by the same family through the years. It had not been rented out until just the last three years due to some family problems.

The kitchen and bathrooms had been updated a few years ago, so the cottage was a delight for the week. Janet did cook some, but they ate out mostly. The one really nice restaurant they had noticed was called Port of Call, it had been there since the thirties but was beautiful inside. It leaned toward the people who had the means to afford high-dollar menus. The menu included everything: Steak,

Seafood and Pork. They offered all kinds of French dishes that looked and sounded great. The décor was velvet and crystal. Janet had thought the restaurant in Roanoke was fancy that Cliff had taken her to, but it couldn't hold a candle to this one. They ate there three evenings during their stay on the island.

The weather was great all week, and they were on the beach for several hours every day. When the end of the week came, both of them were brown with a sun tan. They were careful to always use a lot of sun tan lotion to protect their skin from sun cancer rays.

The cottage turned out to be wonderful, and they decided to put a deposit on it for next summer. They were in luck; when he checked with the agency, he found out that the house was available one week the next July, and Cliff put a deposit down to hold it for them.

Chapter Three

Janet, he spoke. Are you ready to go back to the mountains and start our life together? I sure am, Cliff, she replied and reached over and gave him a long, sloppy kiss on the lips; he enjoyed the kiss and gave her as good as he got.

They had rented the car in North Carolina and knew that they would drive it back to Roanoke. The trip would take them a long day's drive, but they did not want to travel several hours to an airport and then wait for a flight. They enjoyed the drive back up to Roanoke because they took route 460 West, which led them from the beach back up to the mountains. The highway went through rolling hills once they got out of North Carolina into Virginia.

The four-lane divided highway was not overcrowded with cars and almost no trucks and in no time, they had arrived in Roanoke at the airport where they had left their car. Once they had turned in the rental and got into Cliff's car, they headed across Catawba Mountain to little ole New Castle to Cliff's house. She still had her condo in Richmond, but they were going to sell it, and she was going to quit her job and relocate back home to Craig County, where Cliff was still the Sheriff.

Janet was really glad to see the driveway to their house because she was ready to get out of the car and probably turn in early tonight. Cliff, will you get the suitcases and I'll carry the bag stuff in the back seat, she said to her new husband. Hum, Cliff thought, she is already barking orders and making decisions for me! He did as he was told, like a good little husband, but he had decided he would nicely get his way in the future or at least not be told how things were going to be. They were tired and took hot showers and slid between the sheets. Neither was interested in lovemaking tonight, perhaps in the early morning.

They had gone to bed around nine pm, and all of a sudden, both of them were awakened by car horns being blown and the sound of someone beating on a washing tub, or at least that was what it sounded like. Clifford got his revolver from the nightstand and headed down the hallway toward the front door, with Janet creeping along behind him. They had grabbed sweats and shirts and put them on while going down the hall.

Clifford switched on the floodlights that lit up the whole front yard and driveway and slowly opened the door; standing in their yard were at least twenty people banging on metal tubs and others blowing their car horns. What? Cliff thought, Cliff, it is an old fashion serenade. These country people have a custom that when a couple gets married, they do this for good luck for them.

The couple generally gives the women candy and the men cigars. I hadn't thought about them doing this to us, so I hadn't bought anything; then, her mom and dad stepped up on the porch with a bag of candy and cigars for them to give out.

Janet started to open the bag, and her dad stopped her. Wait, girly, there are a couple of things that must be done before the candy and cigars. For good luck, your friends will carry Janet around the house in one of these old-fashioned washing tubs, and then Clifford will be put on that rail that you see Charlie holding over there. Well, Cliff, you get to straddle the pole, and the men will ride you around the house. This is all for good fun and good luck for the two of you. The men came up on the porch and motioned for Janet to get in the tub as they had set it down in front of her. She was a little unsure about this, but she got into the tub.

Three big muscled guys picked the tub up with her in it and put it on their shoulders, which positioned her about six feet in the air and around the house they went. Then, two of the big guys made Clifford straddle the timber, and they went around the house with him, tossing him up in the air, but he managed to stay on the timber.

When those two things were done, all of their friends gave C & J a good hug, and then they issued the candy and cigars to their friends. By the time all this had been done and their friends had left, they had gotten their second wind. They went back down the hallway, but when they reached the bedroom door, Clifford picked her up and took her to their bed, not his bed anymore, and a couple of hours later, they fell asleep in one another's arms.

Chapter Four

Janet awoke the next morning around eight o'clock and glanced at Cliff and she could tell he was still asleep. She put on her robe and went down the hall to the kitchen to put the coffee on. She knew where the coffee and dishes were kept and so she did not make a lot of noise getting this task done. She sat down at the kitchen table while the coffee made itself and whispered to herself, the coffee smells good.

Just about the time she whispered about the coffee, Clifford laid his hand on her shoulder; it scared her because she thought he was still in bed, and she almost hit him with her fist but realized who it was at the last minute. Clifford caught her hand in mid-air and pulled her up out of the chair and into his arms. He kissed her so hard she felt weak at the knees.

Honey, the coffee will have to wait and with saying that, he picked her up and carried her back down the hall and to their bed for another martial round.

An hour later, they both went back down the hall, poured themselves a cup of coffee, and sat down at the table. Janet, what are your plans for today, he asked. Well, honey, I hadn't thought too much about today, but I guess I want to go up to Mom and Dad's and get some of our wedding gifts and bring them over here. Okay, but if you want to wait, we can go over later in the day, in the pickup and get it all with one load. Okay, that works for me she replied. Works for me, too, but I need to go into the office this morning and see what has gone on this week.

They didn't call me, so I guess it was quiet here. I should be back around two o'clock, no later than three for sure. Okay, Cliff, I'll piddle around here. Is there anything you don't want me to get into while you are out of the house? Nah, I am an open book as far as you are concerned; he went out the door, got into his cruiser, and went to the office.

The dispatcher buzzed him in when she saw him walk up to the door. Morning Jill, he spoke as he entered the office. Morning Cliff, well, you don't look too worn out for someone who has been on their Honeymoon! Clifford blushed a little at that but kept on walking and just answered her, yep, I'm on top of the world, as he went on into his private office.

He started going through the mail that had been stacked up on his desk while he was gone. Ah, a letter from Jake Edwards, the FBI agent who was on the Moore Murder case. He slowly opened it, unfolded the letter, and started to read.

Hey Cliff, just a little note:

Thank you for the good job that your office did on the Moore case. Hopefully, it is all taken care of, and we will not have anything popping up, but when it comes to drugs, you can never tell, so keep your eyes open and your nose to the grindstone, just in case something has slipped between the cracks. Old Mr. Harlow will be going to trial soon and I hope they throw the book at him.

Sincerely,

Jake.

Now, that was nice of him to let me know how things were going and thank me for our office's assistance in the case. Hopefully, that ends that. I like Jake, but I hope we don't need him and his team in our county for a long while.

The next letter was a written complaint from a county citizen; it caught the attention of Sheriff Clifford Davidson; what is this going to be, Clifford thought. My name is James Henderson, and I live about halfway up Potts Mountain. I want you to know that I have heard a lot of traffic on this road late at night, and according to car tracks, they seem to be turning off on the Forest road that goes across the top of the mountain.

I felt I should tell you this, just in case something illegal is going on late at night. Clifford went out to his secretary and gave her the letter and asked her to answer the letter with a thank you appreciation note and assure this citizen, that we would be looking into this.

Moving on to the next letter: Dear Sheriff, I just want to write to you and tell you that me and my family think you did a good job in the Moore case. You didn't have a lot to go on, but you came through anyway. Cliff thought for a while and decided that an answer to this letter wasn't necessary.

Sorting through the pile, he found several wanted posters that the FBI had sent to the office. Let's see, a Jill Jackson, last known address, 101 Big Mountain Road, New Castle, Va. Now, who is this? I don't know of any Jill Jackson. Cliff got up from his desk and went out to Deputy Smith's desk and asked if he knew of a Jill Jackson on Big Mountain Road. No, Clifford, I don't recognize the name. Well, do you know what property 101 Big Mountain is? Not right off, but I think Jimmy Jones's address is 99 Big Mountain, so it would have to be after his farm. Okay, I'll just put that on my schedule to drive up there and see what I can find out. Cliff looked at the rest of the wanted posters, and none were anywhere near Craig County; he gave them to his secretary to post on the board so that the deputies could familiarize themselves with the faces, just in case they came across one of them while on duty. He finished the rest of the mail and looked at the call notes. There was nothing he needed to take care of, so he bid his employees goodbye and went home. When he pulled into the driveway, he could see Janet sweeping the dirt off the front porch.

Chapter Five

Well, just look at my little wife cleaning up my dirty porch. Janet smiled and said, don't you mean our porch? Cliff got out of the car, stood up, and loudly spoke, I do stand corrected, my lady. They both laughed, and he jumped up the two steps and gave her a big hug and a kiss on the cheek. Have you had lunch he asked. No, I haven't. Do you? I want to run down to Pine Top for a burger and some pinto beans. Your, on, get in the car, and we will go now, or better yet, let's take the truck, and after we have had lunch, we will go up to your folks and get the wedding gifts.

Sounds like a plan to me, she replied, but I'll have to put on something a little nicer than what I am wearing at the moment. Cliff gave her a good look and finally noticed she was still in her pj's. Okay, I'll be in the truck waiting for you; with that, she turned and went back into the house to change. Cliff went on and unlocked the truck, got in under the steering wheel, and rolled the windows down to get some air.

Janet came running out and jumped down the two steps from the porch to the walk and didn't miss a step until she stopped at her side of the truck. Cliff fired up the old Ford F-150, and they headed down the road to Pine Top restaurant.

Walking into the restaurant, they turned left and found an empty booth to sit in. There weren't many people here at the moment; the lunch crowd had already been, and dinner was a couple of hours away. The server came over with silverware and asked what beverage they would like. She appeared to be a teenage girl but seemed to know her business. She gave them a menu and went to get their drinks. Well Janet, what are you having to eat? It's on me. Hum, I am not sure but I am heading toward a big juicy cheeseburger and a bowl of pinto beans, but I haven't made up my mind for sure. What are you having? I think I want a huge chef salad; they make really good ones here. Yes, they do; I had one a few weeks ago when my parents and I came down one evening.

The server came to their table with their drink orders and asked, what would you like to eat this afternoon? Well, Janet spoke up. I want a huge cheeseburger with French fries. Cliff, what can I get for you the server asked. I want that huge chef salad, please, and would like extra onions and an extra portion of blue cheese dressing. I will put that in right now; give it about ten minutes to be prepared.

Cliff, Janet spoke, you know I need to go down to Richmond and clean out the Condo before I put it on the market for sale. I called the Realtor the other day and asked her to meet me at my place next week on Monday. I need to start going through and weeding out the things I don't want to keep. You know we are going to have to go through your basement and see if we can make room for my stuff that I will be bringing up here.

I don't know what I will be willing to give up. I am sort of a hoarder. Guess what, Honey Pie, you are going to have to make some choices. The Realtor said that most of the old houses that had been split up into Condos, generally bring around $125,000.00 per unit. I sure hope I get something like that. I have owned it for three years and paid $87,500.00 when purchasing it. I still owe about $20,000 on it, but I'll have a little nest egg out of the sale unless my mom and dad want the $50,000 back that they gave me to help buy it. I doubt that they will, Cliff chimed in, but it doesn't matter one way or the other to me. I think between us, we will be just fine. My house is paid for, so we don't have that expense unless we should upgrade what we now have. I will need to have your name added to the deed so it will become ours and not just mine.

I can't foresee a problem if you leave it in your name for right now, but in the long run, you do need to add my name to it just for my protection in case something should happen to you. The server brought their food just as she finished her words concerning the name change.

Wow, does my cheeseburger look good? She grabbed it up and took a big bite out of it, almost swallowing it whole. Gracious Janet, slow down before you get choked; she just gave him a stern look and said: you eat the way you want, and I'll do the same, Mr. Davidson! Okay, Mrs. Davidson, I will, he replied.

Janet did slow down eating. She hadn't realized how hungry she was. They both enjoyed their lunch and, got in the truck and headed home. Do you want to go up to Mom and Dad's for a little while and pick up those wedding gifts before we go home? Sure, he said, as he turned right to head up Town Hill and up the mountain to her folk's place. Within ten minutes, they pulled into her parent's driveway.

Chapter Six

There was a strange car with West Virginia plates on it parked in the drive when they pulled in. I wonder who that could be Janet pronounced without taking a breath. Beats me, Cliff answered, but I guess we are about to find out.

Janet and Cliff went on into the house and found her parents sitting in the living room with a gentleman that neither knew. Janet's mother stood up and uttered that she was glad, that Cliff and her had come over. Janet this is Mr. Henderson. He is with New York Life Insurance Company. He came over to us with the news that your brother had a large life insurance policy, and it paid double for accidental death or in the line of duty. The policy was for $500,000.00, which means the payoff is for One Million Dollars.

Janet took a big breath of air and just looked at her parents in disbelief.

Janet, her mother, continued, the beneficiary is you, dear. The company was having a hard time finding you, so they looked us up as his next of kin. Cliff and Janet just looked at one another with disbelief showing on their faces.

Well, Mr. Henderson spoke up, Mrs. Davidson, the check is written out to you in your maiden name, so I will have to take it back to the office and have them re-issue it in the correct name. You should receive the new check in a week or two. I understand, Janet answered, and at that, he excused himself and left.

Mom, I don't believe what I just heard. I am going to get a check for one million dollars. Why do you suppose John put my name as the beneficiary and not you and Dad's? He asked us about whose name to put on it, and we told him we had all that we needed and that he should leave it to you if something happened to him. We hoped that you would never receive it, but that wasn't the case. Don't you and Cliff feel bad about it? Just know that your brother loved you enough that he wanted you to have it.

Janet and Cliff gave her parents a big hug and went back home. They felt bad about it because they could see the hurt on their faces from losing their only son, and this was just one more thing to remind them of his death. Janet and Cliff hardly spoke a word on the trip back to their place. Neither of them could believe the money that was coming their way.

When they walked in the door, Clifford spoke to Janet and said, we need to talk about what to do with this money, Janet gave him a look of acknowledgment. They settled down at the kitchen table with a cup of coffee and started to discuss the situation. Janet, it is your money, but I feel that you should keep it in the bank, just in case your parents should happen to need it before they leave this earth. But in the end, it is your decision as to what you will do with it.

Janet spoke up, well, Cliff, we are married, and I would suppose legally, half of it would be yours. I do appreciate you taking the stance that it would be mine since it came from my family. I do feel the same way as you; we need to find a good investment for it, and if my parents should need any of it, then it will be there, or if we have an emergency, then we can fall back on the money ourselves. Great, then we are in agreement, and next week, we can go to the bank and see what kind of instrument we can put the money in to earn some interest.

Janet and Cliff had a great weekend. If you call cleaning out the downstairs den, fun. She couldn't believe that a man could hoard so much junk in one room. Clifford didn't have the same opinion of the stuff in the den and she had a really hard time convincing him to part with some of it. In the long run, she won out, as most women usually do.

Monday morning rolled around and he awoke to the smell of coffee brewing. Smiling to himself, because he thought of what he had thought months ago about Janet not minding getting up first and putting the coffee on. He slept nude, so when he pulled the sheet down to get up, he was nude when she walked into the room. Oh, I can see you are up for something, but it isn't coffee at the moment.

An hour later, they went to the kitchen for coffee and breakfast. Janet knew that she would be leaving her Richmond job, but as of the moment, she was on a four-week vacation. Oh, Cliff, I will have to call the Realtor, I was to meet her at my Condo today, and I forgot. I will go down there early tomorrow morning and meet with her in the afternoon. I will stay a couple of days and see what I need to pack up, maybe even pack some stuff. I don't like you going by yourself, but I can't get away from work for a few days. I have made the trip many times by myself, so don't worry. I will give you a call when I get down there.

Janet called the Realtor and changed the appointment to Tuesday afternoon. The next morning, she got up, put the coffee on, and went to the shower and of course, Cliff joined her there. They both had a light breakfast, and Janet got in her car and headed out to Richmond. The drive took about three and a half hours, but it went without any hitches, and she arrived in Richmond on time.

Chapter Seven

Janet didn't like what she saw, as she pulled up in front of her Condo. She could tell that the front door was wide open, so she called 911 and waited for the police to get there. The police car pulled in behind hers and she opened her door and got out. The officer asked for some ID from her and she gladly pulled out her driver's permit that had this address listed. She understood the policeman and why he would want her to show him ID. He told her to stay out by her car, and as he said that, another cruiser pulled up and an officer got out, and both of them went into her Condo.

A couple of minutes went by before the officer came to the porch and waved her to come on in the house. She walked up the steps onto the porch and could see glass lying on the porch floor. The officer escorted her into the living room, and everything seemed to be okay for the most part, except some books and papers had been thrown on the floor.

It appeared as if someone had opened the papers to see if anything was hidden in them and then gave them a toss. When she entered the bedroom, that was another matter. All of the drawers were pulled out, and everything in them emptied onto the floor. When she went into the kitchen, it did not look as if anyone had been there at all.

It took her about two hours to answer all the questions that the police officer asked. The glass in the storm door was broken out, and whoever broke in had forced the front door open. She had forgotten to put the deadbolt on, so at least she could stay here and would have a way of locking the front door since it still worked. The police officers left, and she picked up her phone, called her insurance company, and reported the damage and the break-in. At a glance, she could not see that anything was missing; the only thing that was of value was the revolver, and she had taken it with her for protection in her car.

She dreaded the next call because she had to call Cliff and tell him what had happened. She dialed Cliff's cell phone, and it rang about three times before he picked it up. Hey, I expected you to call me an hour ago that you had arrived safely. I didn't have any trouble on the trip, but when I arrived, I found a mess. What's the matter? He asked excitedly.

When I pulled up in front of the condo, I could see that the front door was wide open, so I called 911 and waited for the police to get there. You might know that since I couldn't come with you, something like this would happen. Cliff exclaimed. Calm down, I am just fine, and there is only some glass broken in the storm door.

The deadbolt still works on the front door, due to my not locking it when I left. I guess that might be a good thing since it will be safe for me to stay here. I can get the glass replaced and the regular lock repaired on the front door. I wish you would just come back to New Castle this afternoon. No, Cliff, I am safe here and want to keep my appointment with the Realtor at four o'clock. Okay, but are you sure you won't come back home today? Nah, I'm good she replied, you forget I have a revolver and know how to use it and will if it becomes necessary.

Okay, but be careful. I will expect you back here Friday afternoon, but I'll call you tonight. Janet went about sorting through the clothes and items on the floor. She was amazed at how much she bagged up to go to the Goodwill Store. She didn't need any of the furniture and hoped to sell it with the Condo. She had bought it all used when she had moved to Richmond, and Cliff's house was already full, so they didn't need any of hers. She had called a Locksmith as soon as the police had gone and he had arrived and replaced the lock on the door. She took the frame out of the storm door and left it at the hardware store for them to put new glass in.

The Realtor arrived at four o'clock on the dot and Janet could see her coming up the walk. Opening the front door, Janet greeted her with a smile and handshake. Hi, I am Mary Jane Johnson, and I am the Agent you spoke with on the phone. I can see from here that you have taken care of the place on the outside.

Janet took her inside, and when they walked into the living room, the Realtor remarked that it was simply beautiful. Walking back to the dining area and kitchen, she was impressed even more. The bedroom was not huge but it would hold most any large bedroom furniture.

It took the two ladies about half an hour to go through the Condo and when she had seen all of it, Mary Jane turned to Janet and asked her what price she wanted for the place. Well, Mary, you're the Realtor, what do you think? Most of the ones here have generally sold for around $125,000.00, but they aren't nearly as nice as yours. I think we should try for a price of $160,000.00, and if we get an offer between the two amounts, then you might want to accept it. That sounds good to me also; I would like for most of the furniture to go with it since I am married and will not need any of it. I hope the offer will be good enough, so I can let the furniture go with the

Condo. Well, Janet, that sounds like a plan to me; she signed the contract that Mary had already filled out and brought with her.

Janet was really pleased; the only thing left now was to give her employer her notice, and she had just enough time to do that. She filled her trunk with all of the clothes in the Condo and drove down to the Newspaper office.

When she walked into the office, her boss hugged her and then asked, where is it? Janet gave him a blank stare and asked, where's what? Your notice, of course, I am surprised you didn't mail it to me, but in-person works. She had written out a notice before she had left the house and just handed it to him with a smile on her face.

Now don't forget, if you write some interesting pieces, email them to me for the paper, and if I think we can use them, I'll send you a check. That's a deal, she said and then told everyone goodbye and started home to New Castle. She was driving west on Interstate 64 toward home and was singing to herself, she felt happy about all of her decisions. She had called Cliff and told him what time to expect her to arrive home. He had been overjoyed to hear she was coming home today.

Chapter Eight

Clifford went to work and told Ike that he needed him to ride up on Big Mountain Road and help him find the address that was listed on the wanted poster that he had received from the State Police Department. The poster had Jill Jackson, living at 101 Big Mountain Road. Ike and Cliff went out and got into the cruiser, and started up New Castle Mountain. It was a horseshoe turn type of road, so their speed was kept down to twenty- five miles per hour until they got to the top of the mountain.

Route Forty-Two was a fifty-five miles per hour road, but if you were not a good driver, forty-five would be a better speed for you to go. Once up the mountain, Cliff increased his speed to forty-five. The turn-off to The Big Mountain Road was a few miles up from the top of the mountain. Here we are Cliff said, when they reached the turn-off to Big Mountain Road. It was a twisting and turning path and a half. You definitely needed to watch what you were doing.

Okay, Ike said to Cliff, that driveway is 99 Big Mountain Road, and the next driveway maybe 100 or possibly 101, depending on how much space the state has given for future home buildings. They drove another quarter of a mile, and then they could see the next mailbox and driveway. There was a white house down a long drive off the road. The mailbox had 101 written on it, so they turned and drove down the lane to the house and barn.

When they approached the house, they could see that it was in disarray on the outside and did not look as if anyone had lived in it in years. There was no sign that a vehicle had come through and mashed down any of the tall grass around the house or barn.

The officers were sure this was a wild goose chase because they could not see where anyone had walked through the tall grass to the house. Clifford knocked on the door once they had reached the porch and when he knocked, the door just opened from the weight of his hand. The officers walked into the kitchen of the old farmhouse and could tell right away that no one had been there in years. There were no appliances in the kitchen, the sink had been removed, and the bathroom had water at some point, but the fixtures were broken up by water freezing in them during the wintertime.

Well, Ike, this seems to be a wasted trip, but I will need to call the state police and tell them that no one has lived here in years, so someone must have misguided them about the address. Ike, I will go to the Courthouse and look up the deed to this property, to see who it belongs to.

Cliff and Ike drove back to town, Ike to his office and Cliff went to the other side of the building to check on the deed to the property. John James, the clerk, looked up the property address for him. Well, Clifford, the property had been sold for unpaid back taxes. One, Jill Jackson is listed on the deed as the owner. Thanks, John. I appreciate the information.

Clifford went back to his office and called the state police office and gave them the news, that he had gone to the address they had and no one lived there. He kept turning it over in his mind; why would anyone in trouble with the law buy an old farmhouse and five acres of land when you couldn't live in the house without some major repairs? The phone rang several times before Sergeant Sizer picked the phone up. This is Sheriff Clifford Davison over in Craig County. I received your poster on Jill Jackson, with an address of 101 Big Mountain Road here in Craig. I have gone to the address, and it is in such bad shape that no one could stay there and I did not find anything that would reflect anyone had been in the house for years. I did go to the courthouse and found out that Jill Jackson does own the property. Sargent Sizer thanked Clifford for checking out the property and advising them of his findings.

One down and one to go, Clifford thought to himself. I probably should wait until tomorrow to go up on Potts Mountain to check out the facts and see if there has been a lot of traffic going into that Forestry/Logging Road. He decided to go back to the office. It was too early to go home.

He pulled into his parking spot and went into the office. The dispatcher told him he needed to call the State Police Office immediately. He went into his office, picked up the phone, and dialed the number. It rang several times, and Sergeant Sizer picked it up again. This is Davison over in Craig County, you had left a message for me to call when I got in the office. Yes, I did. One of our helicopters has been flying over the top of Potts Mountain, looking for Illegal Pot, and when they went by the Potts Mountain Fire Tower, they noticed something hanging from the railings, but the trees were too dense for them to get a good look. We think you need to go check it out. It is probably nothing but a limb off a tree, but we do need to know for sure.

Well, it looks like I need to go up to Potts Mountain; I will be going alone. All the deputies are out on patrol. Clifford got into his cruiser and started his trip. It would only take him about twenty minutes to get to the top of the mountain, but after he turned off route 311 on top, it would take him another twenty minutes to get to the tower itself. At least it is a beautiful day; he thought to himself as he reached the top of the mountain and turned into the logging road.

Logging trucks had left huge ruts in the road, so you had to watch and straddle them, or you would go in deep and need a wrecker to pull you out. He slowly made his way across the top of the Mountain, and now he could see part of the Tower ahead of him, a couple hundred feet, and yes, something was hanging from it. He couldn't tell what the object was until he got out of his car and looked through his field glasses. It had to be several hundred feet up on the Tower to where the object was hanging.

Clifford could not believe his eyes, once he could see with the field glasses, he could tell the object was a body hanging there. He called into the office and had them call the State Police and have them come up here, saying that he needed help with a homicide. He knew it would be a good hour before he could expect anyone, but he got a surprise because one of the troopers stationed in Craig County just happened to be close to him when the call went out.

Clifford had only been waiting about ten minutes when the state police vehicle came up behind his vehicle. He stepped out of his vehicle to meet the trooper. Hey Jay, well, we have another one. What's with this little town? Jay took the field glasses from him and looked up at the body hanging up there. Well, the person was definitely dead for sure. We might as well call in the FBI right now, this Tower is Federal property.

Cliff and Jay waited for the FBI team to arrive, which took them about an hour and a half. To get to the top of the Tower, you had to climb up ten flights of steel steps that led up to the one-room Tower Top, which had a walkway that went all the way around it. Once they got up there, they could smell the body decay and knew it had been there for some time.

The Coroner arrived one hour later and secured the body with a net. He was afraid that it had hung there so long that it might come apart and fall to the ground when they tugged on it to bring it back up to the Tower Top. It didn't and they were able to pull it up and lay it on the wrap-around deck.

The Coroner put the body in the bag and then turned to the officers. I don't know how this person died as of yet, but it would appear from their neck breaking. I can tell you one fact right now: there is a lot of de-composure, but it is a woman.

All kinds of bells went off in Clifford's head when he heard that. Well, I could be wrong, but I bet that this woman is one Jill Jackson wanted by the state police. It took four men to get the body bag down the tower steps, but they got her down. The FBI team was taking fingerprints from the stairway that led up the tower. They probably wouldn't get any good ones if the body had been there as long as it appeared.

The state police and FBI assured Clifford that they would let him know what they found out. Clifford could hardly believe that this was the second murder in this small populated county in two years. He got into his cruiser and headed back into town. Surely, the state police knew more about this Jill Jackson if the body turned out to be hers than they were letting on. I need to call my buddy, Jake

Edwards, at the FBI office and see if I can pry any information out of him concerning this, but I will wait until I hear back that the body is Jill Jackson.

He pulled into his parking place just as his cell phone went off. Hey, you're back already. You're a little earlier than I had expected. I am turning the corner right now, and I'll be in your parking lot in a minute. Cliff, things went a little faster than I expected and so I got out of the city sooner than I thought I would. I got most of what I wanted to keep and brought my clothes with me in the car. I did take a whole load of clothes and household stuff to the Goodwill Store and then went back and packed all the clothes I was bringing back, into the car.

I'll have to call you back; my Realtor is calling me, and I need to answer. Hello Mary, this is Janet, what do you need? Well, what I need is for you to come back and get whatever else you are going to keep from the house. I showed it today and the people made an offer of $175,000.00. I have sent you the forms for you to sign and return to me if this is acceptable to you. You bet it is. How quickly do I need to get what few things out that I want to keep, and when do we close on the house?

The people are paying cash, so we can close as quickly as you can clear out your stuff. They do want whatever you leave in the house; that is the reason they upped the offer from your asking price. This is just great, Mary. I'll talk with Cliff and see when we can get back down. This is Tuesday. I imagine that it is going to be at least Friday before we can get there. Janet, Friday should be okay with the buyers. If you can be here by Friday noon and get your belongings, then we can close around three o'clock that afternoon if that is agreeable with you. That is fine. We will see you Friday unless I talk with Cliff and there is a problem.

Well, I guess you heard the conversation? Yes, Janet, man, this house sale moved fast. When you decide to sell, you sell. Yeah, but I will be glad, come Friday, it will be a thing of the past, and I won't have to think about it any longer.

Chapter Nine

I have news for you. I went up to Big Mountain Road to check out the address of the woman on the wanted poster. No one had been in the house for years, but when I got back to town, I had a call from the State Police asking me to go to Potts Mountain and down to the Old Potts Mountain Fire Tower. Their helicopter had noticed something hanging from the Tower but couldn't get close enough to tell what. Guess what? There was a woman's body hanging by her neck, and she had handcuffs on, and they were cuffed at her back.

I think that the woman is going to turn out to be Jill Jackson, the woman on the wanted poster I had gotten from the State Police about a week ago. She is also the owner of the property at 101 Big Mountain Road. She has owned it for two years, but I could tell no one had been there in years. I did not look at the little Green House that sits next to the road that goes with the property. I need to go back up there and check it out, also. If I remember correctly, there is a little garage beside that house also.

It has been a long drive, and I don't want to go out to eat. That is fine, I'll be home in about an hour unless something comes up unexpectedly. Janet went on home and decided she needed a good hot shower before he got home; the dogs could wait till after she showered.

Things in the house looked okay, she didn't know what to expect since Cliff had batched a couple of days. He could cook, but he was no housekeeper, she had found out. The first time she saw his dirty clothes lying on the floor where he had left them, she had set him straight about that. I will be happy to laundry your clothes for you honey, but I refuse to pick them up off of the floor. If you want me to wash them, then you will put them in the dirty clothes basket in the laundry room. Yes, dear, he answered.

I didn't realize that I was this tired she thought, as she stepped into the shower and the hot water hit her. She just stood there for five minutes, enjoying the hot water running down her tired body. She reached for her washcloth and bar of soap, but Cliff opened the shower door and got the soap and cloth before she could. Cliff, was naked, as a Blue Jay, and he definitely had missed her from the looks of his member. Come on in, pilgrim, she exclaimed! Cliff smiled and did exactly as he was told.

Now that I have showered and don't feel as tired and you have gotten rid of your member problem, maybe we can run down to Pine Top for some supper. Cool with me he answered as he pulled up his pants and buttoned them up. They went on to Pine Top and walked in and saw their good friends, Josh, and June Taylor, so they sat down at the big table with them after they had been invited, of course, and enjoyed a great meal and had good company along with it.

Clifford got a meatloaf dinner, and she ordered a shrimp dinner. She knew it would be frozen shrimp, but in the mountains, that is about all you can expect. If it were frozen fresh, it should have a good taste.

The Taylors had been in Craig for some time and lived a couple of doors down from them. They were nice people, and all four enjoyed one another's company.

Not that anyone needed dessert, but they ordered pieces of

homemade German Chocolate Cake. Cliff loved it and devoured his in about a minute, so Janet pushed hers over in front of him. She had taken several bites, but she told him it would look better around his waist than hers, and then all four of them gave a hardy laugh.

The couples sat and ate and laughed together for almost two hours. It was a good thing that the restaurant wasn't so busy, or they may have asked them to hurry up and eat so someone else could have the table.

Cliff and Janet got into their car and Janet slid over next to him, used the middle seatbelt, and snuggled up close to him for the ride home. She was quite content with her head on his shoulder, and he liked having it there. They hadn't been married very long, but each day brought them closer. I will check my schedule tomorrow and make sure I can get off to go with you to Richmond, not that you need me to go. Just think I would like to go with you. That's fine with me. Just tell them your wife said they had to get along without you for the day.

Chapters Ten

Friday rolled around rather quickly, and Clifford had arranged to be off. Being the Sheriff, he could be off anytime since he was his own boss and was an elected official. Cliff was not the kind of person that would take advantage of a job such as his. He believed the people elected him to do a job, and he needed to be there to see that it was done, either by him or one of his deputies.

They decided to take Interstate Eighty-One to Interstate Sixty-Four. This route is a little longer mile-wise, but the speed limits on both are Seventy, so you get there in less time. They arrived at Janet's condo around ten a.m. and Cliff went through the items with her and loaded them in the pickup. He figured everything wouldn't fit in the truck cab, so he brought a tarp along with them so he could cover the items in the back of the pickup and sure was glad he did; once he was in the house and saw the boxes that she had packed up to bring back to New Castle. They got all of them stacked in the truck and tied the tarp over them so that if it rained on them traveling back, nothing would get ruined.

They arrived at the Realty office right at two o'clock and sold the Condo, got their check, went by Janet's bank, and deposited it. The time was getting late, so they thought that they should grab something to eat before hitting the Interstate back home. There was a Longhorn Steak House just down the street from the Reality Company, so Cliff turned into the driveway of the steakhouse. I hope this is okay with you, he asked. Yeah, it's fine. I could use a good Ribeye, and they have good ones here. Clifford came around and opened her door for her, and gave her a hand to help her out of the truck. Janet blushed a little, she was not used to having doors opened for her. She wasn't a Women's Libber; she wanted her man to show her attention, so she enjoyed being treated like this. They were seated in a nice booth by the window where they could see the parking lot from where they had been seated and could keep an eye on their truck.

The server came over with silverware and napkins. How may I help you this evening he asked. We both will have regular coffee, black, with no cream or sugar, please. We know what we would like if you want to take our order now. Okay, he replied and got his pad out. They had iPads and put your order in at your table. She would like the twelve-ounce ribeye, cooked medium with baked potato, extra butter, no sour cream, and a tossed salad with blue cheese dressing. I will have the Porterhouse, well done with potato and salad, the same way as hers. He had input the order as Cliff had told him and smiled and said I'll be right back with your coffee.

Well, honey, how does it feel to be a free woman? Cliff, it feels really good. I am now a kept woman. Hum, that means you will have to treat me real nice when I ask! Baby, you won't even have to ask, and I'll be so nice you may not be able to stand it. They both laughed so loud that they were afraid they had disturbed the other guests. The server brought them their coffee, and they both lit into it. I needed a pick me up Cliff touted, same here was her reply. They had some easy conversation until their food arrived, at which time they lit in on it and did not talk hardly at all.

They walked out of the restaurant on full, and Cliff wasn't sure if he would fit under the steering wheel. He hadn't realized how big a

Porterhouse is. Honey, we will have to play the radio loud on our way back to keep me awake; I feel like an old bear full and ready to go to sleep. I will keep an eye on you then. I don't want to be in a car crash tonight.

With that, he hit the on-ramp to I-64 and sped up to seventy miles per hour. They had gone about twenty miles and were out of Richmond and moving along the countryside; traffic was light and moving right along. All of a sudden, Clifford could see headlights coming up behind him and he could tell by the way they were gaining on him that the vehicles were moving at a fast rate of speed.

 Hold on, Janet, I may have to turn to the shoulder in a hurry. There is a car driving at a high rate of speed coming up; about that time he went over in the pull-off lane at seventy miles per hour. He was able to keep control of the truck and slow it to a stop. He kept his eyes on the cars, it turned out to be two Mustangs racing. He quickly called the State Police Headquarters, which he knew was a few miles up the road from them. The phone was answered by a woman. This is Sheriff Clifford Davidson of Craig County.

Two Ford Mustangs racing just forced my wife and me to the side of I-64. One is red, and the other black, both look like new models. I would appreciate it if there is a trooper near us if they could try and intercept them. We are at milepost 25 and the vehicles in question are headed west from us. I hope you can stop them before they kill someone. Thank you, Sheriff. I will see if there is a trooper ahead of you and have them pull over and wait to see if the cars pass them doing the speed you are talking about; with that, the woman on the phone hung up the phone.

Cliff and Janet calmed down, pulled back onto the interstate and picked up their speed to seventy again. They had gone another ten miles and rounded a curve, and sure enough, there were the two Mustangs with cruisers with lights flashing.

One in front of the Mustangs and the other behind. The troopers had the two young girls outside of their cars, and Cliff could see they were handcuffing them. See Janet, those young women were exceeding one hundred miles per hour. That is an automatic arrest charge. You can bet they are going to have one hefty fine when they go to court, not to mention they will have to post bail to get out of jail. They went on and finally got to where they took I-81 south, down to Roanoke, where they would take the New Castle exit onto State Route 311 that led them to New Castle. They arrived home at eleven o'clock safe and sound and were ready to hit the bed.

Janet got up at six thirty the next morning and put the coffee on. She knew he would want some as soon as he awoke and came into the kitchen. Funny, she thought, how soon people start to get used to their partner's habits after marriage and are together all the time. She could hear Cliff coming down the hallway; she sat down on the kitchen chair, pulled her robe down off one shoulder, lifted one leg, and draped it over the chair arm.

Once she had done those things, you could see half of her breasts and not quite her bottom, but not much of it was covered. Cliff walked into the kitchen wearing his robe. Darling, she said, trick or treat. I'll take the treat, please, mam! She got up out of the chair and jumped into his arms. Well, we all know what happened then. He didn't get his coffee until later. They finished their breakfast and then went out to unload her belongings from the pickup. I hope all this stuff will fit down in the den in the space we have cleared out for it. I think it will; this is stuff that I don't want to get rid of. They carried it all down to the den, and sure enough, it all fit.

Now, the den was full of stuff and they just had little aisles to walk between the rows of stacked boxes. Clifford, we do need to get down here with a serious thought on getting rid of some of this mess. One of these days, we may want to use this room for what it was built for! A den for watching TV and playing around in. Clifford looked at her with an inquiring look and finally spoke. Janet honey, I do want children, but not quite this soon. I hope you are not implying that you are pregnant or that you want to start a family. Gosh, that is a no on both of those questions. Yes, I would like a child or two, but not for a while. I realize you are a few years older than I am, but not that many.

They finished unloading, and Cliff told her that he needed to go into the office and check things out. Yes dear, she patted him on his butt as he went out the door. He turned and gave her a quick cheek kiss as he left. He walked in the door and greeted the woman behind the desk that had buzzed him in.

Walking into his office, he tried his best to think of the dispatcher's name. He had hired her to dispatch two weeks ago, but her name just wouldn't come to him at the moment. Sitting down at his desk he could see a pile of calls he needed to return, but nothing bad had happened while he was away. He was glad. It seemed that every time he was away, something out of the ordinary happened. Flipping through the notes he could see most of them were already taken care of. His buddy from the FBI, Jake Edwards had called and asked if he could come over whenever Clifford had returned to work. He picked up the phone and dialed Jake's number. After about three rings, he picked up. Jake Edwards, how can I help you? Hey, this is Clifford over in Craig, I came in today to see what had happened while I was gone and see that I have a note to call you. Yes, I would like to come over one day and have a conversation with you. How about tomorrow we can go to Pine Top and have lunch, I know that is why you like to come over to Craig.

Jake laughed and confirmed the appointment at noon and yes, he would like to go to lunch. Clifford hung up the phone and finished looking at the stuff on his desk. Going back by the woman at the desk, he spoke, you doing okay, June? He had thought of her name just then. I'm fine, Sheriff, how about you and Janet? We're just fine. I am heading back home now. Give me a call if something comes up that you need me for. Will do, Sheriff, have a nice afternoon she said. Clifford drove his car back to his house, and when he arrived, he found Janet on her knees scrubbing around the commode in the main bathroom. What are you doing, he asked. Well, I came in here and took a good look and could see that you don't have very good aim while using the commode, I decided that this would be my project today since you were gone. Okay, but we can get someone to come in and do this deep cleaning. She turned and gave me a look. I don't think so, at least not as long as I am able, and I hope that will be a lot of years to come. She just turned around and continued her scrubbing. I will be through here in just a little while; just sit down and be a good boy.

The doorbell rang, and Clifford got up and went to the door; opening it, he saw Janet's parents standing there. Come on in, I'll get Janet. I came home and found her scrubbing the main bathroom floor. Hey, honey, your parents are here. Quit what you are doing, and come on in here. He could hear her footsteps coming down the hall. Hey, Mom and Dad, what do we owe this visit to? Well, my darling daughter, her father spoke. I was missing your smiling face, and your mother and I decided to just pop in for a few minutes.

Her parents visited for about an hour and then excused themselves and left. They had a good visit but after they left, Janet looked at Cliff and said, something is up. My parents did not act normal, and I think they wanted to tell us something but, for some reason, could not bring themselves to do it. Janet went back to finish her cleaning and he went outside to give his car a good wash job.

Cliff came back into the house about an hour later and went to their bedroom and found Janet taking a shower. He returned to the kitchen and got himself a cup of coffee. In a few minutes, Janet came into the kitchen after she had finished her shower. Clifford spoke up at once, dear since you were the cleaning lady today, would you like to go into Roanoke for some dinner this evening? I think that would be rather nice of you, my dear, she answered him, with a smart aleck tone in her voice. Okay, let me go take a shower and get some clean clothes on. He went down the hall and dropped his clothes on the bedroom floor and got into the shower. He was singing a song to himself when she opened the shower door and stepped in to join him. Well mam, what do I owe this pleasure to? Well, Sir, it would be my pleasure to help you clean up, I did a good job on the bathroom, so let's see what I can do with you, but mam, you just had a shower. I will need another when I am done here, was her answer. With that, she gave him a hard, sloppy kiss, and that was all it took to get Clifford ready to go.

They stayed in the shower until they had used all of the hot water, and it started to turn cold on them. Cliff turned the water off, reached outside the shower, and got a bath towel off the rack. My dear, let me dry you off, and then you can do the same for me. They both helped one another get dressed and started down the hallway just as the phone rang. Janet picked it up and answered Hello, this is Janet. May I help you? There was a pause and then a click and now just a dial tone. I guess it must have been your girlfriend; they hung up on me. Yeah, right, that is all he could say. He did not like her making a comment such as that.

They drove into Roanoke and decided to go to a little place called Sassy's. The restaurant was small and was run by a nice couple; she did the bar and he was the cook. They had two other women who waited tables and doubled at the bar. They only purchased good grades of meats, and they had the best prime rib and steaks in the city. The strange part was they didn't charge an arm and a leg for their dinners. Clifford told the waitress they both wanted the prime rib special, baked potato, and salad. She brought them the glass of wine that he had ordered when they first came in and sat down. The wine was really good. It was called Liberty Creek Sweet Red. Janet did not care for the dry wines; they were too sour for her taste, but she liked this one.

They had a delicious meal, and it took them two hours to finish eating, but it did not seem as if they were being rushed to get through their meal and leave like some restaurants make you feel. Cliff thanked them for a delicious prime rib as he paid the bill. By the way, the owner said we have sold the place, and the new owners will be taking over next month. That's good for you I am sure, if that was what you had planned on. What kind of restaurant will it be? Cliff asked. It is going to be an Irish Pub, offering Irish drinks and meals. It will be something different for this area for sure. I hope they make a go of it. Me too, Cliff answered, well, we will miss this restaurant for sure, but good luck in whatever you decide to do next. With that, they left the restaurant and headed back to New Castle.

Chapter Eleven

They started back to New Castle and were headed down Catawba Mountain when he noticed a car appeared to be following them or it seemed that way to him. He sped up to sixty mph, which is about as fast as you can travel safely on Route 311, and he did not want to drive recklessly, so he didn't go any faster. Sure enough, the driver of the car behind them had increased his speed also. Janet don't get excited, but I am not sure if the car is following us, but I'll pull over down the road and let them go on past me.

He reached down and got his revolver from under the seat. Janet, I'm going to pull off the road to the left and if I tell you to duck, then lay over in the seat quickly. Okay, but why? Just do as I ask, and don't ask questions right now. Cliff gave his signal, turned to the left to a wide space, and stopped. He could see the car behind him had stopped even with him, and the driver's window was being lowered.

Layover, Janet, right now, she did as she was told. The window in the other car came down, and Clifford lowered the passenger window on his car to prepare for what was about to happen. The driver of the car that was sitting in the road stuck a shotgun out of the window, and when Clifford saw this, he rolled over on top of Janet, put his pistol out of the window, and started firing, hopefully in the right direction of the perpetrator. He heard tires cry on the pavement when he began firing his weapon. He could tell that the vehicle had left, so he set up and helped Janet up.

Janet, are you okay? Yes Cliff, but what was that all about? I don't know, honey, but I plan on finding out. They were both lucky; Cliff thought, I must have hit the driver when I fired for him to have left without firing off the shotgun. He got his cell phone and immediately called into his office.

Craig County Sheriff's office, the woman answering the phone said. This is Sheriff Davidson. I have been ambushed by a man driving a red Ford Mustang and he took off in the direction of New Castle. I am right at the Craig/Roanoke County line, so he will only be able to turn up West Craig Creek Road or come on into New Castle. Send a deputy toward me, and maybe he will pass him on the way out of New Castle. I will wait at the turn-off to West Craig Creek for the deputy, and if he doesn't see him before he meets me, we will know he is probably headed up West Craig Creek Road. Deputy Smith is headed out right now. He was here and heard everything you said, so he will be looking for that Mustang while on his way. Cliff turned into West Craig Creek Road and pulled to the side of the road. It took Deputy Smith about ten minutes to get to their location. Clifford got out of his vehicle and went with the Deputy up West Craig Creek. He told Janet to go to her parent's house and under no circumstances to go to their house. Janet did as she was asked and went to her parent's home just for safekeeping. They were surprised when she rang their doorbell, do, to the late hour. Her mom answered the door and asked, honey, what is wrong?

Nothing, Mom, well there is, but I don't know what at the moment. Mom, Cliff, and I were ambushed on our way home, and he does not know why. He sent me on here till he can get back home. The car that was going to shoot at us sped off toward New Castle after Cliff emptied his service revolver at them. He thinks he may have hit the driver with the shotgun because they never fired the gun and just sped away.

Ike and Cliff went up West Craig Creek Road until it ended up at State Route Four-Sixty, just outside of Blacksburg, Va., but they couldn't catch up with the Mustang. Ike, the car could have turned off several back roads. If he knew Craig County roads, he would know that he could turn off West Craig Creek and go over the gravel road that leads over Hall Mountain Road and it would put him back on Route Forty-Two. He could get out of the county down that road. Clifford picked up the car phone and called the office.

Send a deputy up Route Forty-Two; we want to make sure the car that ambushed Janet and me is not doubling back. Yes, sir, I will send Deputy Jacobs. He is just pulling in from making his rounds. Ten-Four, Clifford said and hung up the phone.

Ike, just head down Four-Sixty and turn back onto Forty-Two. I doubt we are going to see the car, but we can try. Ike and Clifford turned back onto Route Forty-Two and proceeded east to New Castle. They met Deputy Jacobs when they were about halfway back to New Castle, but neither had seen the Mustang. It doesn't surprise me. Cliff said, thanks, guys. Ike just take me to my in-law's house. I sent Janet there and not to our house. They went on the back road and finally pulled into the Moore's driveway. Clifford's car was in the driveway, and all the lights were on in the house. Thanks, Ike, Cliff said as he shut the door of the cruiser. Janet came running out of the house and jumped into Clifford's arms.

Sorry, Janet, we did not see anything of the Mustang, but I called the FBI and appraised them of what had happened. I am sure Jake will call in the morning and when he does, I think he and I are going to have a very serious conversation. Janet just looked at him but didn't say anything. She didn't know what to say because she had no idea what was happening. Clifford had tried to get her to stay with her parents and not come home until tomorrow, just in case the men came back and tried something at their house. She flatly refused that idea and got into the car.

He had been married to her long enough to know not to try and change her mind. Once she had it made up, there was no turning back. He was glad to see no odd cars near his house or in his driveway. They were pulling into their driveway when his cell phone went off, Clifford here, he said as he pushed the answer button. Clifford, this is Jake Edwards. I got your message. I need to come over tomorrow for a meeting with you, but I do need to tell you to be very careful due to what just happened to you. I will explain what I know tomorrow to you, be careful and goodnight.

Well, Cliff, what was that all about Janet asked. Honey, your guess is as good as mine, but I will say I think it has to do with Miss Jackson. He didn't say to her what he had been thinking ever since they had found that woman hanging from the tower. Let's get some rest now, and maybe tomorrow, when Jake comes, I will have something more to tell you.

Chapter Twelve

The alarm went off at six thirty, and Janet slid out of bed and walked into the kitchen. She made a direct beeline to the coffee maker, poured the water into the tank, dropped the lid down, and turned the warmer on. Clifford had not heard the alarm go off, so she would have the coffee made and if the smell didn't wake him, she would go shake him out of the bed. She knew he had that meeting with Jake Edwards today, and she wanted him to be on top of things when it happened.

The coffee brewer started its moaning and groaning, letting her know it was done but Cliff hadn't come into the kitchen yet. She went down the hall and into their bedroom, and when she entered the room, she could hear the shower running. I would like to surprise him and join him, but this morning just isn't the right time. Hey Cliff, the coffee is done when you get out of the shower. She could hear a muffled okay out of the running shower, so she went back to the kitchen, poured herself a cup of coffee, and sat down at the table. Cliff came meandering into the kitchen fifteen minutes later and had only a towel wrapped around him. Man, I am sleepy today, he said, as he poured himself a cup of coffee and sat down at the table. The towel gapped open as he sat down, but he didn't try to hide anything, and it came falling out of the front of the towel. Janet noticed but did not say anything. She just wondered how she could have been so lucky to snag a man who was so kind to her and was endowed like an elephant. What is that smile on your face he asked, oh, nothing she answered. She would like for him to carry her off to the bedroom, but she knew today, or at least this morning, was not the time.

She fixed him some bacon, eggs, and toast, some honey in case Cliff wanted some on his toast. She wanted just toast and maybe some honey on it this morning. They sat and ate in silence until finally Clifford ate his last bite and looked up at her and, with a smile on his face, said, Honey, I'd like to take you back to bed, but I just have too much to do today. She smiled back and answered, I know. I had already thought about it after you came in here half-naked, but I know that today you have a lot to take care of, so don't think anything about it. I'll take a rain check, please. She got up and gave him a sweet, gentle kiss on the lips.

Cliff went back to the bedroom and got into his uniform and told her goodbye and left for the office. When he pulled into the parking lot of the Sheriff's office, he could see that Jake was already there. Man, he is early. He must have something urgent he needs to talk to me about. The dispatcher buzzed him in and told him that Mr. Edwards was waiting in his office.

Morning Jake, you sure are early this morning, you must have something really important to tell me or a lot of important stuff to tell me, which is it? Both Clifford and some of it you are not going to like for sure. Well, bad news doesn't get any better with time, so just tell me and get it over with. Clifford, I am afraid that the John Moore case may not be over because of the current things that have happened in the county. We definitely got the right person for his murder, but the drugs coming into Craig County have not stopped. We feel that old man Harlow, who is in prison now, is somehow still in charge of the drug running in this area. We have looked into all of his visitors and so far, he hasn't had any. Nowadays, prisoners can have cell phones, and unless you can prove probable cause, you cannot put a tap on their phones.

We have done some digging into Harlow's business affairs, both legal and illegal. We did find some things that were overlooked before. One thing was that the woman that you found hanging from the Fire Tower was associated with him. The drugs are a part of a Cartel out of Mexico, and we think that Jill Jackson's death may have been connected to the Moore case. I know this is going to rub salt into the Moore's wounds, and I am sorry, but it looks like the case will be reopened. I do hope that John Moore's family will not have to be involved in any way.

When we first checked out Miss. Jackson's death, we thought it was a homicide. We have fingerprinted all of the railings on the tower steps and the handcuffs that her hands were fixed behind her with, and the only print that we came up with was her own. We have come to the conclusion that she took her own life by affixing the rope around her neck and then putting the handcuffs on her wrists, and then taking a leap off the tower to end her life. She was mixed up with the Drug Cartel and was afraid of what they were about to do to her because of the money that they had lost.

Jake, do you think that the attempt on Janet and my life last night is a part of all this? Yes, I do, Clifford and we are digging deeper into all of the aspects of this case, trying to find a missing link that would help us to end all of this. Cliff, until we can come up with something, you need to be extra careful. It is hard to tell what a Mexican Cartel might try up here in the mountains. We did check out the property belonging to Miss. Jackson, but there was no sign of anyone being there lately. Maybe she had bought it on behalf of the Drug Cartel and they were going to use it like they did the North Side Farm. You're probably right about that, Clifford; just keep track of what might go on up there.

Jake, I really appreciate all this information and will instruct my deputies accordingly. I just don't know how Janet and her parents are going to react to this news. I am sorry, Cliff, but we just don't have any other way of dealing with this.

Clifford finished looking at the paperwork that had piled up on his desk and then went home to tell Janet the news he had received from Jake. Janet met him at the door as he opened it to enter the kitchen and grabbed him and smiled at him and then a hug. He smiled back and held her until he felt her back away. She gave him a know-it all look, that women sometimes have and then asked? Cliff, what is it? He just stood there and tried to think of the right way to tell her the news. I hate to just blurt this out, honey, but there isn't any way to tell you but just directly. Jake informed me this morning that they were going to re-open your brother's case. Janet's mouth just fell open but he just continued telling her what he had been told by Jake. Cliff ended his conversation, and Janet just stood there in disbelief, with her mouth still open and a tear starting to form on her eyelid.

I am sorry honey, I wish I could have broken the news easier, but there wasn't any way. Jake did say, he hoped that your family would not have to get involved. I hope not. I don't know if my dad could take it; he and my brother were really close.

He told Janet what the FBI was about to do, and he thought she had handled it, well, he just hoped her parents would handle it as well as Janet. Cliff went into the kitchen and poured himself a cup of coffee and sat down at the table. Janet came in, and with one look at him, she could tell that he was in deep thought. A penny for your thoughts, honey! Well, Janet, I am worried about us being ambushed, and I just don't know where to start to find out who is behind everything. I did report it all to the FBI, and maybe they can help out. I am sure they will, Cliff. Try not to worry so much about it.

Chapter Thirteen

Monday rolled around, and Clifford went into his office as usual. Deputy Smith met him at the doorway of his office and followed him in. Cliff, your buddy Jake at the FBI, called earlier and asked if you were going to be in today and I told him as far as I knew you would be. Thanks, Ike. If he doesn't call me in a few minutes, then I'll try calling him back. Okay, Ike replied as he went through the door into the main office. Clifford threw himself into his paperwork and before he knew it, two hours had passed by. He picked up his phone and dialed Jake's number. Good morning, Jake Edwards speaking. May I help you? Yes, this is Clifford Davidson. I was told that you had called earlier and I am returning your call. Thanks, Clifford; I have some news, hopefully good, on this end.

We put out an APB on the Red Mustang, and the deputy in Giles County found a Red Mustang with bullet holes in it and blood stains on the steering wheel. It looks like you did indeed hit the driver, who was about to fire his weapon at you. Unfortunately, the Mustang had been reported missing, in Rockingham County yesterday. We did get a tip from someone, near where the car was hidden in the trees that they saw a white Toyota leaving that area several hours after you reported your situation. They said that it had New York tags on it, but they couldn't get the number itself. The witness got the first three letters on the plate, and it read TOY. We are running a check with New York now to see how many tags they have starting with a TOY. It's like looking for a needle in a haystack, but we have to try.

Clifford was still bothered by the decision the FBI had come to, that

Jill Jackson had killed herself, and he had decided that he would go back up to the Tower and look around himself. He did not think that he needed anyone with him, so he drove up to the Tower alone. Going very slowly down the old logging road to avoid the ruts, he came to the Tower before he knew it. The logging trucks had left huge ruts in the road and if a smaller vehicle got into them, they would have to be towed out with a wrecker. The Tower was a couple of miles off the hard-surfaced road, and it took about twenty minutes to get to it. Cliff finally reached it, pulled his cruiser to a stop, and got out.

He looked at his watch as he started to climb the first set of steps, and it read one o'clock on the dot. He reached the top of the first flight and caught his breath. Man, I only have eleven more flights to go up and each flight has thirty steps on it. Cliff got to the top where the Tower Room was, and he had to stop to catch his breath. He had not paced himself and by the time he had gotten to the top, he could hardly breathe.

Standing at the top you could see for miles in all directions. He wondered what the men who built the tower thought when they finished building it in the year of 1912. Thinking to himself, what a beautiful view this is, and then he decided that it had not been a nice one for Jill Jackson. Walking around the outside platform to the point that Miss Jackson's body was found hanging from the metal railing, he could tell the metal was beginning to rust badly. The U.S. Forest Service did not use these towers any longer, so they did not do maintenance on them. He had bought his camera with him so he could take pictures of anything that he found that he thought was not as it should be.

He was looking at the outside wall of the enclosed room and could see scuff marks on the metal side opposite the area where Miss. Jackson leaped. The walkway that he was on had a wide railing at the top that a person could stand on to leap off the Tower. He took a picture of the scuff marks on the building that he found and turned around to examine the railing itself.

On a closer look at the railing, he could not find any evidence that anyone had used the side of the railing to climb up on top to jump. He took pictures of the railing sides and then looked at the top. The top was about six inches wide and a person could stand on it, but nowhere on the flat service could he find any marks in the rust coating that was on the metal. If someone climbed up there, they would have had to disturb the rust coating and they had not. He took a picture of the top. Once he returned to his office, he would download them to his computer.

The old road that he took to the Tower kept on going and, circled down the mountain and came back onto the main road another five miles below the Tower. Clifford decided that he would continue on the logging road until it came back onto route 311. He slowly wound his way down the mountain, maybe a couple of miles, until he came upon a car that had gotten into the deep ruts in the road. Stopping his cruiser behind the vehicle he got out and walked up to the vehicle. He noted that it looked to be a very new Ford and had New York tags on it. Upon looking at the tags, he knew something was up. He returned to his cruiser and called into the office for them to send a deputy and a tow truck. He knew it would take them at least an hour to get to his location, so he got into his vehicle to wait for them.

He had been late going to sleep the night before and he nodded off for a few minutes and woke up to the sound of a vehicle coming up behind him. He could tell that it was a diesel truck and, on this road, probably a four-wheel drive. He could not see the vehicle yet, so he decided that he would leave the area and meet up with the deputy and tow truck further down the road. The hair on his neck was standing up, and that was his way of knowing things were not right at this moment. He started his cruiser and drove around the car and was able to go on down the road until he reached the deputy and tow truck just as he arrived at the main road turn-off. The deputy and Clifford took up positions behind their vehicles. They could hear two vehicles coming down the road toward them.

Clifford had called in the State Troopers for assistance because he was pretty sure this was related to the drug cartel and John Moore's death. The state police arrived on the scene about two minutes before the big truck and the car, which had been stuck in the ruts, arrived near the law enforcement roadblock.

The truck and car stopped about fifty feet from Clifford, opened their doors, and slid out of the seat of the truck behind the doors. Clifford knew what was about to happen, just as he had finished thinking this, the gunfire erupted. There appeared to be two guys, one driving the truck and the other from the car. They exchanged gunfire, but there were five laws, to two bad guys, so the bad guys lost the battle in a hurry.

They walked up to the guys lying on the ground, and right away, they could tell that both were deceased. Clifford could see that the big pick-up had Maryland license plates. Once the gunfire had stopped and they had checked out the two dead men, the State

Troopers took over the scene and immediately called in the FBI. Well, maybe they will be able to pin some identification on these guys and shed some light on things. When the FBI arrived, Clifford could see that Jake was among them and went directly to him so that he could tell him what had happened. Jake and Clifford discussed what had happened, and then Jake told Clifford to go back to his office and that he would keep him appraised of what happened once they could examine everything. Clifford did tell Jake that he had gone over the hanging scene and that he did not agree with the FBI's findings. Jake wasn't pleased with his findings, but he said he would check them out once he got back to the office and could look over what the FBI had reported from the scene of the hanging.

Clifford drove back to his office, sat down at his computer, and downloaded the pictures he had taken. He then noted all the findings he had come up with, or no findings, in the missing marks, where a person would have used the railing to climb up on. Once he was finished, he sent Jake an email with his write-up and the pictures. They could not say that he was not diligent in his work. Once he had finished, he bid his fellow workers goodnight and went home to Janet.

Chapter Fourteen

When he pulled into the driveway, he could see that Janet was not at home because her car was missing. He thought she was probably at her parents, house, he dialed her cell number, and she picked up on the second ring. Cliff, where have you been? I expected you home a couple of hours ago, but I did not call the office. I knew you were busy, or you would have come home. I will tell you what has happened when you come home. I am heading in to take a good, hot, long shower.

Ending the call, he went into the bedroom and stripped off his clothes, dropping them on the floor. The light bulb went off in his head, Dummy, you had better pick the clothes up and put them in the dirty clothes or you are going to catch you know what. He did not blame her for taking a stand; she was his wife, not his slave, and he just loved her more for being the way she was. Once he finished his shower, he felt so much better and thought he might just live now. Turning on the TV in the kitchen and flipping the coffee pot on, he sat down and waited to smell the coffee brewing. It only took a couple minutes for the pot of java to brew, and he got up and poured himself a cup, went into the living room, and sat down in his recliner.

Janet came strolling in about an hour later with a big smile on her face and a fresh apple pie in her hand that her mother had made. Hum, let me have a piece of that hot pie to go with this coffee, please, oh please sweety pie. She went to the kitchen counter and cut him a piece about the size of a fourth of the pie. Honey while you eat your pie, I will run and take a shower, okay, he said between bites of the pie, I'll be right here.

She returned thirty minutes later and got her a cup of coffee and sat down beside him. Cliff reached over and ran his fingers threw her long hair and smiled at her. Honey, I have something to tell you and hope it doesn't cause you to be very sad.

Today, I went up to the Tower to check things out myself, and when I had finished looking things over, I decided that I would take the long way around the Mountain Top Road. I had driven a couple of miles when I came across a car that had gotten into the deep ruts that the wood trucks had made. To make a long story short, other people were coming to get the car out, and they were not nice people. I had to call the State Troopers in to help me.

There was a shoot-out, and both men that caused the problem ended up dead on Potts Mountain. Jake Edwards told me that they were going to re-open your brother's case because the drug cartel is still involved here in Craig County. He believed the woman's death on the Tower is associated with the cartel and probably your brother's death also.

He could see the hurt in her eyes as he told her about what had happened. Cliff, will my brother's death ever be over? Each time my parents and I get a little closure, something else comes up. I don't know how much more we can take. He put his arms around her and gave her a long, strong hug until he could feel her pulling back. I know you care, Cliff, but it is going to take me a little while to get this wrapped around my head again. I don't think we should tell my parents about this until something more happens. I agree, Cliff chimed in. They don't need any more grief than what they already have at the moment.

Clifford went into his office the next day and immediately called Jake. Morning, this is Clifford, do you have any ideas on what happened yesterday up on Potts Mountain? I am not telling you how to run your business, but I have a feeling in my gut that the two men who died yesterday are connected to the Moore case and probably were working from the orders of one Mr. Harlow out of his prison cell. Clifford, you are probably correct, but right now I am having to wait on the court system to allow me to put a tap on Harlow's phone.

Until then, I am afraid my hands are tied. I hope that in a few days, I can get the authorization that is needed to proceed. Until then, I am trying to find out who the two dead men are. We are running a trace on the two vehicles that we have from Potts Mountain. We are pretty sure the sedan is a rental, but the truck does not appear to be one. We have asked Maryland to run the tags and see what comes up. The man did not have any ID on him, nor was there a registration card in the truck.

Well, Jake, I hope we get a break in this case faster than we did with Moore's death. I hope so, too, Clifford, but we just have to play the hand that we are dealt. Your right, Jake, but sometimes it seems like the hand of the law is the one that gets smacked more than the lawbreaker. Clifford thanked Jake for his update and hung up the phone. He proceeded to download his pictures and comments into his computer from his phone.

He got that part done in about ten minutes. As he looked at each picture and wrote comments concerning them, he couldn't help but see the fingerprints in his photos. He had taken several of the railing where the woman supposedly jumped and had climbed up on the railing. This bothered him to no end, even after he had finished downloading all the pictures. It was only two o'clock, and he felt like he had the time to go back up to the Tower before dark fell. He slowly drove down the road to the Tower to avoid the ruts. Climbing up the many flights of stairs leading up to the Tower Top. He carefully took more pictures of the fingerprints, and then he took his fingerprinting powder and brush out and did the old fashion way of getting prints. He did, however have a machine to send them to the database at the FBI for them to run to see if they had a match.

He returned to his office about an hour after he had sent the prints to them. There was a fax lying on his desk when he sat down. The fingerprint that he had found had been overlooked by the team who had printed the tower during the woman's death. They had run the print, and they had not found a match in their system, but they had entered it into their records and would let me know if someone matching was entered later.

Chapter Fifteen

The clock struck five o'clock, so Clifford locked up his desk drawers and headed home. When he arrived home, he could see that his in-laws were there, and he was all right with that. He had grown to like them. He went up the front steps, and when he got to the door, Janet opened it up and, with a big smile, gave him a big kiss. They went on back into the house and Cliff found her parents sitting in the kitchen, both with a big mug of coffee. I'm sure you guys haven't been piggy with the coffee and drank it all up, I could use a cup. Janet told him to sit down with her mom and dad, and she would get him some. She had made a fresh pot, and it had just finished brewing. She returned, put a mug in front of him, and then sat down in her chair next to him. Well, Moore's, what do we owe this pleasure to? He called them the Moore's instead of Mom and Dad. Janet's dad started by saying, you can call me Dad if you like. That is what Janet calls me. Okay, Dad, Cliff replied, with a big grin on his face, to which Dad returned his smile.

We did come over wanting to talk with you and Janet, so we waited for you to get home. Okay, Cliff said, with a somewhat puzzled look on his face, what is it you want to tell us? This may come as a surprise to you, but Janet, your mother, and I have decided to leave here and go to Florida to live. We think all of our old bones would feel better down there in the heat. Janet is now our only child, so if you want our house and property, we will sign it over to you two. We do not need the money from a sale of it and would rather you take it and enjoy it if you two would rather live up on the mountain than in town.

Janet and Cliff just sat there for several minutes with their mouths wide open, not knowing what to say. She could hardly believe her ears. Was she hearing her father correctly? Now, Dad, let me get this straight: you and Mom are leaving Craig to go to Florida, and you are giving Cliff and me your property. Yes, Janet, that is exactly what I just got through telling you!

Cliff spoke up, Dad and Mom, are you sure about all this? Of course, we would rather live on your property. It is much nicer than this one, but what if we decide to move somewhere else in the future? How would we work things then? That is not a problem, Cliff. Once we sign it over to the two of you, it is yours to do as you please. We are not filthy rich, as the saying goes, but we do not need the money that the sale of the property would bring.

Mom, have you and Dad decided where in Florida you are going? Yes, and we have even bought a beach Condo on Hutchison Island in St. Lucie County. The place is about fifty miles north of West Palm Beach. The weather is going to turn cold shortly, and we want to get everything taken care of and go to Florida at the last of October. We are not going to take anything with us besides our clothes and golf clubs, so get prepared to have yard sales or take the stuff to the dump. We are leaving everything in the house for you to keep or toss.

Cliff and Janet stayed up another hour discussing what they needed to do with her parent's things and then went to bed. Since they would own both places, they could take their time tossing or selling the items in both houses that neither wanted. Her parent's home was much larger than Cliffs, so she would keep a lot of stuff for the moment. Cliff could see the handwriting on the wall, he knew how much stuff she could hoard up like he had any room to talk!

Neither Janet nor Cliff slept much that night; both kept going through their minds what they needed to keep and what to toss or sell. Finally, around four o'clock, both of them fell asleep in each other's arms. The alarm clock went off at six thirty, and Janet rolled out and went down the hall to make the coffee. Cliff was awake when she got out of bed but did not say anything. He just let her think he was still asleep. He lay there for a few minutes and then got up and showered and dressed. He went down the hallway, into the kitchen, and straight to the coffee pot. It was ready and there was a mug sitting next to it for him. Pouring him a mug full, he wondered where Janet was. He sat down at the table about the same time she came up from the basement. She gave him a stern look and said, Clifford Davison, you are going to have to get rid of some of that junk down in that den, period! He didn't like what she said but felt that he should keep his mouth shut for the time being. That would be another war to be fought another day.

The next morning rolled around really fast. It seemed to Clifford that he had just put his head down on his pillow when he heard the alarm go off. Janet slid out of bed and went and put the coffee on as she always did each morning, she felt like she needed to do this for her hubby. Cliff came stumbling in ten minutes later, rubbing his eyes, stopping long enough to give her a pat on the butt and a kiss on her neck.

Well, Cliff, what's your day going to be like, she asked. To be quite honest, I don't know. I have some usual stuff to do, but I am hoping Jake will call with information about the vehicle owners that we took in off Potts Mountain. I am sure he will let you know, just as soon as Maryland lets him know. Yes, I know you are right. I need to be more patient in these situations. Cliff went back to the bedroom, put on his uniform and came back through the house and told Janet goodbye.

He got into his cruiser and went on to the office, hoping that he would hear from Jake concerning the car they had found and who it was that had tried to kill him and Janet, and hopefully, some information on the vehicles on Potts Mountain.

Morning Rose, things are quiet in the office today, he spoke as he passed her while going down the hall. Yes boss, quiet as a mouse so far, but you know how that goes. Oh yes, I do know, but we can hope for the best out of people anyway. He went on down the hallway and into his office. Taking a seat at his desk, he could see several notes lying on his desk that needed his attention. Picking up the first one, he could see it was not urgent, so he laid it down just as his phone rang. Morning, Clifford Davidson speaking. Hey Cliff, this is Jake. We have gotten a couple of breaks in the re-opened Moore case. Just this morning Maryland got back to me on the vehicles up on Potts Mountain. The car was a rental, and a man by the name of S. G. Zimmerman had rented it two weeks ago. I am running a rap sheet on him as we speak. The white truck was owned by one, T. A. Zimmerman, both guys lived in the Baltimore area.

The other break is that a hunter found the body of a guy not more than a mile from where we found the car that had ambushed you and Janet. We are running his prints now and I will keep you informed as soon as I hear something. Hold on a minute. They just laid some information on my desk.

Well, the Zimmerman guys on the mountain are brothers and are known for drug running in Maryland, but the authorities there could never pin anything on them. However, the authorities did confirm that they had their suspicions, that these guys were connected to our Mr. Harlow. I just got the ID of the dead man up on forty- two. He is one Eric Taylor, also from the Baltimore area, and is the son-in-law to S. G. Zimmerman. Clifford, it looks like we are putting the puzzle together concerning the drugs in Craig and who is behind them. The dead guy had two shots to the head. I am sure if we check your revolver, the slugs will be a match. You are one good shot. You couldn't even look where you were firing. Just plain dumb luck is all it was, Clifford replied. They chatted about some of the other things about the case and then ended their call.

Clifford remained at his desk for the next couple of hours until it was lunchtime. He asked Ike if he would like to have lunch with him. Sure, Clifford, I am hungry. Are we going now he asked. Yep, I am hungry also, so we can just head out right now. I think I would like to have one of those huge hamburgers at Pine Top. I think that will stop my stomach from growling like it has been doing for the last hour. They got into the police cruiser and headed North to Pine Top Restaurant. When they entered the restaurant, they saw another officer of the law sitting alone at a table. Clifford wasn't bashful, so he went to the table, introduced himself and Ike, and asked if the officer would like to have some company for lunch. The officer was a little surprised at Clifford's take-charge attitude but answered, sure, please sit down.

Once they were seated, he introduced himself. I am Charles Warren, and I work at the Botetourt County Sheriff's Office. I lived up on

Meadow Creek and was coming home early and since my wife is gone for a few weeks visiting family, I stopped to have some food before going home. I am afraid I am not much of a cook, or at least I just won't cook if I can get out of it. Ike and Clifford both started laughing at this point, they knew just what this guy was saying; neither of them would cook as long as there was a restaurant near to get a meal.

Charlie seemed to be a nice guy, he and his wife had not been in the County long. They had rented a place on Meadow Creek just a few weeks ago and so far, they loved living here. He asked Clifford about the body on Potts Mountain. Being a police officer, he was interested in what was happening, especially since he was living in the county now.

Clifford found out from their conversation over lunch that Charles and his wife, Julie, had been married about six months and children weren't in the plans as of yet. Julie was in California visiting relatives for a few weeks but would be back before Christmas. They had rented a house on the back road across from where Janet's parents lived and where he would be living in a few months.

They shook hands, and Charles went on his way, and Ike and Clifford went back to the office. Clifford took his seat at his desk upon his return from lunch and started looking at the paperwork that had appeared while he was gone. He thought if I didn't have to do paperwork, I could get more police work done. Shuffling through the papers, he could see some wanted posters hot off the press at the bottom of the pile. Pulling them out of the pile, he began to look through them. He did not see any of them that should have any effect on Craig, so he gave them to the clerk to post on the board for the deputies to familiarize themselves with. He wished that the FBI could get a match on the fingerprint he had found on the Tower railing the last time he had been up there.

Chapter Sixteen

I am not busy today, let me call Janet and see if she would like to ride up to the Tower and we can enjoy the afternoon together, and I can also look around the Tower again. You never know what you might find when you are not looking.

He picked up the phone and punched in Janet's number. It rang about four times before she answered. She seemed out of breath when she answered, so Janet, why are you panting? I was in the basement den when the phone started to ring, and I had to come up the steps running. I'm not eighteen anymore, so I can't rush quite so quickly. How would you like to ride up to Potts Mountain Tower with me this afternoon? I would love it. I am tired of digging around in that den. I could use some fresh air. I will be there to pick you up in fifteen minutes; this is a go-as-you-are trip; don't change into anything. Your work clothing will be just fine. Cliff pulled into the driveway exactly fifteen minutes to the second to pick her up. He came into the house and pinched her on the butt, and went to the bedroom to change out of his uniform.

This is an unofficial trip, so I don't want to be wearing a uniform or driving a county car. They went to the old truck, once he had put on civies, hopped in, and took off in a cloud of smoke. The old truck needed valve seals in the engine, and when it sat for a few days, oil would leak into the cylinders; when someone started it up again, the oil would burn up in the cylinders, and smoke came out of the exhaust pipe. It was a little embarrassing, but adding a little oil every few thousand miles was cheaper than the fifteen hundred dollars that the garage wanted to put tiny seals on the push rod entries. He didn't use the vehicle that much, so he could not justify the output of that much money to keep it from belching smoke out now and then.

The drive up to the Tower is beautiful from New Castle to the top of Potts Mountain, it is the prettiest 15 miles that you can drive and see gorgeous scenery. The logging road that you go along the mountaintop lets you see over both sides of the mountain, one side. You are looking at a pristine mountainside that runs down to Paint Bank, where the Country store and the Swinging Bridge Restaurant are located. There is an old hotel that has been remodeled and a train depot that has been turned into an inn. They also have a couple of new tent rooms that are becoming popular now. You walk into a room-sized tent, and inside, there is a beautiful bedroom suite and bathroom. This sets out in a field next to a creek that is flowing off the mountain and has trout swimming in it. The only thing you have to be aware of is the black bears that may come around looking for any food you may have left out.

Cliff had some friends who had rented a cabin about a mile away from the tent for the week. The second night they were there, a bear came up on the porch and threw the grill they had used that day down into the yard. The bear could smell the food that had been cooked on the grill and was after it. The couple had put a dresser in front of the door to make sure the bear couldn't force its way into where they were. They left the next day; they weren't taking any chances that the bear might come back to visit another night.

Cliff and Janet had gotten up to the top of the mountain and were about to turn down the logging road. Both of them could see something stretched out across the road as they reached the top. Cliff slowed and then stopped, in front of the truck was a huge rattlesnake crossing the road in front of them. It had to be at least six feet long and as big around as two garden hoses. Janet was afraid of it, but Cliff just said, we need to wait a minute and let the old gentlemen finish crossing the road. You have to remember we are in his home, so we need to be a little respectful of his habitat. The old snake made his way across the road and down the bank into the woods, and they continued on their journey to the Tower.

It took them about fifteen minutes down the logging road to reach the Tower location. It was a beautiful spot and would have made a good picnic spot. He switched off the engine, and Janet and he got out of the truck and walked over to the Tower bottom. What are you looking for she asked, not for anything in particular, just anything lying on the ground that shouldn't be there. Just walk slowly around the yard of this rusty tower and see what you can find lying on the ground or maybe even partially buried in the ground. There were a lot of people up here because of that woman's body, and if they missed seeing something and stepped on it with heavy boots on, they may have mashed it into the ground and not even known that they had.

Yes sir, boss, I'll do that right this instant, she replied to him with a smile on her face. He knew she was just being cute for his benefit and did not mean anything ugly with the comment. They both moved around the yard. It was grown up, so it would have been easy for any of the officers to miss a clue lying on the ground. Janet was taking her foot and moving it sideways on the grass so that she could see down in the tall part to the flat ground. Even looking in this manner, it was difficult to see down in the tall grass, but suddenly, she could see something glistening in the sunlight. She called Cliff to come over. She knew not to touch it, let the law man do his thing. He came over and cleared the grass away from the item she had found. He had a box of gloves in his truck, so he went and got a pair to pick up the item that she had found and also a plastic bag to store it in. It could turn out to be a possible clue to the woman's death, which he thought was murder, not suicide. He took a sterile wooden tongue depressor and dug the item out of the dirt. The item turned out to be a pretty new hunting knife with the initials CCC engraved on it. Cliff gently put it in the evidence bag and sealed it up.

Gosh, Janet, you do good work. Next time I have to go over a crime scene, I will just call you in to do the search. She smiled at him and said, anytime, if you want something done right, just call a woman! They kept on searching the yard for another hour but did not come up with anything else except some old tin cans that hunters had thrown down many years ago.

They got in the old truck, and Cliff told her that he was going to go down the way he had the other day when all the ruckus took place. Janet enjoyed the ride over the top of the mountain and down the steep road that led them back to Route 311. The road came back out to the main road about ten miles from the Tower. She did not see any bears on the way down the mountain. However, there must have been at least fifteen deer in the woods as they came down. They did not move; the noise of the truck didn't bother them. It is said, that they know when hunting season is in, and once people start shooting at them, is when they get all spooky and run from every noise they hear. The couple enjoyed their outing on the mountaintop; the weather was nice, and it had been a balmy sixty-five degrees. When they reached the main road, Cliff looked at her and asked, would you like to go back over the mountain to the restaurant at Paint Bank and get some supper? It is only four thirty, and they don't close until seven, so we have time.

I would love to, but look at my clothes. I have dirt all over me. I think we had better just go home. I would not feel right going into the restaurant looking like this. Yes mam, he said, your wish is my command, and took a left at the main road and headed back into town. She jumped into the shower as soon as they got back to the house from their mountain trip. Cliff had gone to the mailbox and gotten the mail and was sitting at the kitchen table when she came down the hall once she had finished her shower.

When he looked up as she entered the kitchen, he was pleasantly surprised. She was wearing nothing but a thin nighty top that you could see through. Well, honey, I can see what you have on your mind and not on your body. I can take the hint, and I am game for a wild romp if you are. She came over to him and sat down on his lap. He could smell the soap scent on her body that she had used in the shower. Gently, he helped her out of the nighty and started caressing her neck at the base of her head, moving slowly up her slim, long neck, using his moist tongue to massage her neck. She would quiver each time he had stopped and then started again. He could tell that she was really in the mood for some wild sex in the bedroom. When he took a break from her neck, she got up and turned to him, unbuttoned his shirt, and removed it from his body. She also had a talented tongue and started using it on his chest, and when she got to his hairy chest and tits and massaged them with her hot tongue, he thought he might not make it to the bedroom. He became aroused instantly. Picking her up and carrying her back to their bed, he placed her gently on it and crawled in with her. Kissing her hard on the lips and then running his moist, hot lips all over her body until he could tell she could not take any more foreplay. She wanted him inside of her because she had grabbed him and pulled him on top of her, telling him to get down to business. He pleasured her for two hours before both of them were exhausted and just lay there in a heap of hot, sweaty flesh. They both fell asleep and did not wake until the doorbell started ringing.

Janet jumped up and put on the clothes she had worn to the mountain and went to the front door. She could see her Mom standing on the porch. She opened the front door and greeted her. Honey, I hate to bother you two, but I was in town and started home, and my car sounded terrible, and I was afraid to go home in it. Just as she finished telling, about her car, Cliff came to the living room where they were standing.

Mom, I can go out and see if I can tell what is happening. Tell me what the noise sounds like. When I put on the brakes, it sounds like I am rubbing two pieces of metal together. That sounds like your brake pads are worn out to me. Let Janet take you home, and I can take your car to the garage and Janet can pick me up when she comes back down the mountain. Sounds good to me, Cliff. I hate cars when they act up. I have been telling her father that I need a new one. I think this one has over 100 thousand miles on it. Janet and her mom got in her car, and she started up the mountain. Cliff waited about twenty minutes and then got in her mother's car and took it down to the local garage. The brakes squealed every time he applied them, which told him she either had dirt between the pads and rotors or the pads were gone. More than likely, the pads were worn out since the car had that many miles on it.

He pulled into the garage parking lot, and he could see Jack standing in one of the bays with his body stuck under the hood of an old Chevy. Cliff walked into the bay and hollered Jack's name as he came through the door. Jack came out from under the hood and came back with, hey bud, what's up with you today? I have brought my mother-in-law's car in to have you look at it, she was down off the mountain and was too afraid to try and take it back up the mountain due to the noise the brakes were making. The car has over a hundred thousand miles on it, so it is probably the brake pads. Sure thing, Clifford. I will have a look at them and give the Moores a call tomorrow and see how they want to proceed with the repair. Clifford talked with Jack a few more minutes before Janet came rolling in to pick him up. She gave Jack a wave hello, and Cliff jumped in the car, and she took off to their house.

Thanks a lot for helping my folks out, I know you didn't have to, but you are a nice enough guy and hubby that you wanted to help me out with them. Not a problem, I will help them out any time I can.

Chapter Seventeen

As they went on back to their house, it was starting to get into the evening hours and the sunlight was starting to dim. Clifford went in, stripped down, and got in the shower; the hot water feels so good running down my body. I may stay in here for an hour or two, or at least till I use all of the hot water out of the heater. He would rather Janet come in and wash him down, but he didn't think that was going to happen this evening. He did the necessary things, dried off, dressed, and started down the hallway. He met Janet coming down the hallway. She gave him a big smile and informed him that she was coming in to see if he had drowned in the shower. Dinner is almost finished. I hope you like grilled cheese sandwiches and soup. It's cool, I like both of them and am ready for some food in my stomach. They went into the kitchen and took their seat at the table; Janet had already put the food on the table, and the steam was still rolling off the soup bowls.

Clifford lit into his sandwich and soup like he had not eaten in a month. Cliff, slow down before you choke on your food, she uttered. He came up for air, lay his spoon down, and smiled at her. It is so good, honey. I just wanted to keep shoveling it in my mouth and chewing.

They kept on eating and talking, and before they knew it, their bowls of soup and sandwiches had disappeared from in front of them. They continued sitting at the kitchen table and began to discuss the den and all of the stuff that was stored down there. Cliff, honey, you know that some of that stuff is going to have to depart from this house and not go to the new one. Yes dear, I know, but you also need to take a look at what you have here that you are willing to part with. Well, Cliff, do you want to go down right now and start sorting through some of that stuff? We will have to begin in the closest corner and start two piles, one for keeping items and another for throwing out.

They went down the steps and into the den. Cliff had a sad look on his face as they reached the bottom of the steps. Okay Cliff, look at this pile first. Right on top, you have an old baseball glove. It looks like it has seen better days. It is still usable, but Cliff, you don't play ball anymore! All right, we can take it to the Goodwill with some of the other items we are bound to decide to get rid of once we get into tossing. She went into the storage room and found a large empty box, brought it into the den, and gave the glove a toss into it. That's one down and a few hundred more to go she exclaimed. Cliff chimed in with, and all of them will not be just mine! They stayed in the den for the next couple of hours, and when they quit, there was a large Goodwill box setting in the basement, and a wide area of the floor was now open space.

I am proud of you, Cliff. You have shown some really good maturity today. We have begun to clean out this house, and we both know this house has to be gleamed first. I know what you are saying and I am doing my part, but when we get over to your stuff, I want to see that same maturity from you. You will, my dear, just wait and see! I am going to hold you to that, my dear, we will continue this tomorrow evening. The two of them climbed back up the steps and sat down at the kitchen table with a cup of hot coffee in each of their hands. Cliff got up from the table and smiled at her, well, dear, I have taken one shower today, but now I need another one since I got sweaty from the downstairs work.

I may need some assistance since I am tired from all the work. She just smiled and waved him on. Get on in there, she exclaimed. You're a big boy now. He went back to the bedroom, dropped his clothes, and stepped into the shower. He had picked up the soap when he heard the shower door open, he turned around smiling. He knew that she would be coming because she liked their episodes in the shower as much as he did. She took the soap and washcloth from him, lathered up the cloth, and started washing his back slowly and very gently. She knew what was taking place at the front of his body. That was her intention all along. Clifford turned to her, and they enjoyed one another for half an hour before the hot water turned cold on them. Man, I am going to get a new water heater so our interludes can last longer; please do, Janet chimed in. They had been married for six months now, and every time Clifford touched her, she quivered all over and was ready for him to take her. She hoped that this feeling for him would never end, and she knew he was having the same reaction and hoped that always want her this badly.

Chapter Eighteen

Monday morning rolled around fast once more; again, he thought, man, the weeks and months are passing by quickly. The alarm went off, but she didn't move, so he got up and went into the kitchen and put the coffee on. As usual, he was stark naked. After all, it is my house and if I want to walk around this way, it is mine and Janet's business. He went back to the bedroom and into the bathroom to shave and do the other necessary things. He was almost dressed when Janet stirred and slid out of the bed. I am sorry, honey. I did not hear the alarm go off, or I would have gotten up and fixed the coffee. That is okay. I still know how to pour the water into the maker. They both laughed at that. She knew he appreciated her thinking enough of him to get up and do the kitchen thing while he got ready for work. He finished dressing, and she put on her robe, and they both went to the kitchen. She fried him some sausage and eggs with some toast to go with the coffee. They enjoyed their breakfast, and Cliff went to his office to begin his day.

Clifford let himself into the office door with his key. He could see that the dispatcher was not at the desk when he walked up to the door. Things were very quiet as he entered the hallway and started to his office. He could hear a weird-sounding noise as he went down the hallway, but he could not determine what it might be from the sound he was hearing. He went into his office and decided he would like another cup of coffee, so he went into the hallway and started for the breakroom. Walking through the breakroom door, he could see Julie, the dispatcher, lying on the floor next to the stove. He ran over to her and kneeled down to her. One glance, and he could tell she was alive but not able to respond to him. He pulled out his Cell Phone and called The Life Saving Crew, which was located two blocks from the office. He would have dialed 911, but the dispatcher lying on the floor was the person who would have answered the call.

The crew was there in ten minutes, but Clifford had to leave Julie to open the door for them to come in. They rushed to the breakroom and started checking her vitals immediately. She began to come around while they were working with her. Where am I? She asked. Oh, I know what happened. I was here at the coffee pot, and now you're sitting me up. The crew captain asked her how she was feeling now and if she could remember coming to the breakroom. Yes, I wasn't feeling quite right and thought, I need some sugar of some sort. I am a diabetic and was feeling faint. They checked her sugar level and found that it was on the low side but was climbing up to normal. Your sugar fell too low on you, Julie, and you passed out. Yes, she replied, I know better than to wait when I feel faint, and I have life savers in my purse just for that reason, but I did not want them. I wanted coffee with sugar in it. Next time, I will just get the Life Saver.

The time had flown and by the time the crew left, two deputies had arrived, and also the new dispatcher to take over the new shifts. Julie was okay by the time the crew left and she went on home.

Now that all the excitement was over, Clifford was able to go back to his office and start his day doing the Sheriff's duties. He picked up the phone and dialed Jake's phone. Morning Clifford, Jake answered the phone saying, morning to you to Jake. I am calling you because Janet and I rode up to Potts Mountain Tower on Saturday afternoon and were looking around, and we found, or should I say she found, a hunting knife in the grassy area around the Tower. It is a Sheffield with the initials CCC cut on the handle. Since it is a really expensive knife, we might just be able to find out who the owner is and how he lost it at the Tower. The only place I know you can buy them around here is at the knife store at Valley View Mall in Roanoke. I think that you can buy them online, but they are shipped from England, and the freight you have to pay makes this type of purchase a little too expensive for the normal Joe Doe to afford.

That is logical, Cliff, but you never can tell what people are willing to part with their money for these days. I will run over and pick it up sometime today. Will you be in the office? I should be unless something comes up that I am not aware of. I will give you a call if I need to go out somewhere. What time do you think you will come over to Craig? Let's plan on me being there around ten o'clock, if that is good for you. Okay, I'll expect you around that time unless you call me to cancel. He hung up the phone and started going through the mail on his desk. Today, there wasn't that much, thank goodness; when he picked up the third message, he was intrigued by how it read. Dear Sheriff Davidson, in my opinion, you are the worst Sheriff that Craig County has ever had since I have been living here. Clifford smiled to himself.

At least once a month, he would receive one of these letters. In the beginning, it bothered him, but after a couple of years, he did not let it disturb him anymore. He gave it a toss into the trash can, picked up the next letter, and began to read. The phone rang, and he stopped to answer it. Morning, Sheriff Davidson speaking, may I help you? Janet spoke to him, morning dear, so what have you done this morning? Something good, I hope. Oh! Nothing spectacular; I've just been going through the hate letters and talked with Jake about the knife. He is coming over in a little while to pick the knife up so the FBI can run tests on it. I am not sure when he may arrive, so I am pretty sure I won't be home for lunch. That is okay. I am going to Mom's, and we are going to go through one of the bedrooms and see what can be tossed or given to the Goodwill. That sounds like a good plan, honey. I'll see you this evening when I get home.

Clifford finished up the rest of the paperwork and then went back to the breakroom to get a cup of coffee. Julie was sitting at the table when he entered the room and gave him a good morning. Julie, what are you doing here, he asked. I was going home, but I remembered I was supposedly pulling a double shift, so I came back, I was feeling fine after I got over my episode with the sugar. When I came back to the office, the other dispatcher was already there. I think I was just confused about my schedule. I am getting some hot coffee before I start back home this time. I can tell you that you gave me a scare this morning when I found you lying on the floor. I am sorry. I will try not to do that to you again anytime soon. He smiled at her, picked up his coffee, and went back to his office.

Looking at his watch, he saw that it was ten to ten, and he knew Jake would be Johnny on the spot right at ten o'clock, so he picked up his coffee cup and finished it off. Jake came in right at Ten; Clifford spoke, I knew you would be here right on the dot. Yes, he replied. I try to be on time wherever I need to be to take care of business. I do also, it is just the way I am. I can't remember when I didn't have this attitude. Here is the knife. Clifford pulled it out of his desk drawer as he spoke to Jake. Here it is; I used gloves and put it in this protective bag, just in case it turns out to be connected to the case.

Thanks, Clifford. I should have known you would know how to handle evidence. I did a little bit of digging concerning the knife but didn't find much. There is a store in the Valley View Mall that does sell expensive knives like this one, it is called The Hunting Store. I know the store, Jake replied, and I went in it to see what they had when I was at the mall. I will go by there as I go home this morning and show them the knife and see what they say. Okay, I hope you have good luck with it, Cliff replied.

Jake stood up and bid Clifford goodbye with a handshake, and went out of the door. Clifford saw Julie go by his office. As she was leaving the office, he called out to her goodbye and said that he would see her tomorrow.

Hey Clifford, I am going to Pine Top and pick up a burger, would you like for me to get you something? Yes Ike, I would like a cheeseburger and fries, if you don't mind. I don't mind, I wouldn't have asked you if I did. Ike went on out the door and to Clifford, it seemed like he had been gone five minutes when he came back in and set the lunch down on his desk. How much do I owe you, Ike? It came to $8.95 with tax. Clifford gave him a ten-dollar bill and told him to keep the change as his part for services rendered. Ike just gave a hard laugh and kept on walking out of Clifford's office.

Cliff tore into the burger like a madman. He hadn't realized how hungry he was until he had taken the first bite. He had just finished his lunch when the phone started ringing. Wiping his hand to remove any grease from the burger, he picked up the phone.

Hey, this is Jake. I just left the knife store at the mall. They have no record of selling this to anyone. They seem to think that it may have been ordered online from a major store in England, especially since it has the initials cut on it. They are going to put a request in and see if they can find a name for whoever bought one and had the same initials monogrammed on it. It will take a while, but they have my number to call when they get an answer. Sounds good to me, Jake. I will be looking forward to hearing from you on this. It was now almost five o'clock, so he decided that he would call it a day and go home.

He could see Janet's car in their driveway as he pulled off the street. I wonder what is for Super, he thought as he opened the front door. She was in the living room and was all dressed up, sitting in her chair. Well, hello, he uttered to her, and a good evening came back from her. I am afraid to ask why you are all dolled up. Honey pie, my parents are taking us out to eat as soon as you get changed. I am to call them when you are ready. I would have called you at work and given you fair warning, but I knew Jake was there, and I did not want to disturb you.

I don't need a shower, but I will go change into civilian clothing, so you can go ahead and call them, I'll be ready by the time they get here. He went down the hallway to their bedroom to change his clothes, and she reached for the phone to call her parents.

Her parents arrived about half an hour later and just honked the horn for them to come on out to the car. Cliff opened the back door to the F-150 and helped Janet up into the back seat and then jumped in himself. Evening people, Cliff chimed in, where are you taking me to eat, somewhere expensive, I hope? I could use a Twenty-Ounce Ribeye and a baked potato weighing about a pound with butter running out of it. Gosh, Clifford, Mrs. Moore exclaimed, you had better watch all that cholesterol.

Chapter Nineteen

The four of them rode into Roanoke and went directly to the new Longhorn Steak House that had just opened at The Valleyview Mall. Janet and Cliff had not been there yet, so the choice her parents had made suited them. The hostess seated them in a booth that gave them a little privacy, which they were glad to have gotten. Their server came over and took their drink orders. The Moores wanted regular coffee, but Cliff wanted a beer and Janet just water with a lemon wedge. He left to get their drinks and was gone about three minutes before he returned. The four had looked at the menu and decided what each of them wished for dinner. Mrs. Moore wanted a small sirloin, medium well, and Mr. Moore ordered a twelve-ounce ribeye. Janet wanted the same as her mother, but Cliff ordered the twenty-ounce T-Bone medium well.

Clifford, when you get as big as an elephant, you will have to sleep in the guest bedroom. I don't think our bed can handle a Four Hundred Pound, man, she smiled as she made the statement. She knew he could eat as much as he wanted and never gained an ounce. The server went to put in their orders, and they began to talk about the Moore's upcoming move to Florida. You know Cliff spoke, the two of us are going to miss you guys when you leave. Janet's mother spoke up, that will give you a good reason to come down to Florida and use our guest room. Our Condo is located on the beach road; you can have your coffee on the screened porch and watch the water lap on the sand at the shoreline. That does sound great, Janet told her mother. How soon can we come?

The server brought them the food and the Chef had prepared everything just as they had requested it be cooked. Finishing up his steak, Clifford thanked his in-laws for the wonderful dinner that they had provided. He was most welcome, his father-in-law replied. Clifford offered to leave the tip, but Mr. Moore would have none of that. This is our treat; enjoy and be quiet, he said, with a smile. Clifford knew to just accept and be quiet. He liked his in-laws but had learned to just let them have their way as long as it didn't matter.

In the conversation, he had learned that Janet would be helping her mother go through the rest of the house this week and they would clear out the items that neither wanted to keep. For most of the items it did not matter to either as to what happened to them. It was decided that Janet would retain all the family pictures here in New Castle. She would have lots of room in her parent's house and they would not be in the new Condo in Florida. They would take one good picture of their late son and one of Janet and me on our wedding day. Clifford was dreading the day that her parents got into their car and started down the road. They had already given Janet her mother's car; it had too many miles on it, and they would get her mother a new one in Florida.

They did not have a use for the car, so they had asked permission to give it to an older couple in the county who needed a newer vehicle but could not afford to purchase one. Her parents were thrilled that their old car was going to be a Godsend to someone who needed it.

The couple also wanted the living room suite that Clifford had in his house. Janet's parent's furniture was much newer and Janet and Cliff would keep her parents. Janet's mother had every kitchen appliance that anyone would want and was not taking any of them.

They would take what they were using to the Goodwill, along with another six pickup truckloads of her stuff. They might just leave the bedroom furniture in Cliff's house and let it go with the sale. The next three weeks had Janet helping her parents clean out their house and Clifford making trips to the Goodwill to drop off loads of items that neither couple wanted.

The big day had finally arrived, and Cliff and Janet were on their way up the mountain to see her parents off. Clifford was not looking forward to this day, but maybe Janet and her parents would handle it okay. Clifford was starting around the last curve at the top of the mountain when, all of a sudden, there was a four-wheel drive truck coming directly at them. He could not let the two vehicles collide; the truck was much larger, and the outcome for him and Janet would not be good. He did the only thing he could do, jerking the steering wheel to a hard left. He went to the other side of the road that the truck should have been on. The truck hit the back end of their car as they swerved to keep them from being head-on. When this happened, it made their car turn around twice and the back end slid over the embankment.

The car came to a halt with its back end sticking over the mountainside; the only thing saving them from going over and down the mountainside was the front end of the car, which had landed on a huge rock that was positioned on the side of the road to help people from driving over the side of the mountain. Neither he nor Janet were hurt, but they got out of the car as quickly as possible. He did not think it would finish going over the mountain, but if it did, he did not want them to still be in it. It had to be at least a hundred feet drop before you landed in the tree tops below. They climbed out of the car and when he looked down the road, he could see the pickup in the ditch, but there was no one getting out or standing near it. Janet, you stay here. I will call the office and have them send a trooper and an ambulance. I am afraid someone is hurt in the truck. He called the office as he walked to the truck. When he got close enough, he could see someone slumped against the truck door. He opened the passenger door and could see a woman, who must have been driving the truck, lying against the door. She was ashen white and was not breathing. He could tell by her looks that she was deceased.

The trooper arrived on the scene about the same time he had opened the truck door. The ambulance came just a few minutes after the trooper. The medical people examined the woman and found out that she was deceased, and there was nothing they could do to help her. The trooper called the Funeral Home to bring a Hearse to pick up the body. Clifford reached and picked up her pocketbook, and he found her wallet just inside it. She was Jackie Short and lived in Giles County, just over the Craig County Line. He did not know of any Shorts that lived in Craig, but that could be her married name. Janet walked down from their car just as the Hearse arrived and they were pulling the woman from her truck. She could see the woman's face and made a gasping sound, Honey, do you know this woman, Cliff asked her. Yes, I do, she is my girlfriend's sister, and she lives up Sinking Creek in Giles County. I need to call your girlfriend to let her know what has happened. Is this lady married? If so, we need to call her husband. Clifford looked into her purse and found a card with next of kin listed with a phone number. Clifford dialed the number, and a child answered, is your daddy at home? I need to talk with him. Clifford didn't tell the child who he was. He didn't want to upset the child.

Suddenly a man's voice came on the phone, this is Jack Short, who is this? This is Sheriff Davison in Craig County. I am afraid I have some bad news for you. My wife and I were coming up New Castle Mountain, and on the last turn at the top, we met a pickup on our side of the road. We managed to avoid a head-on, but the truck hit the back end of our car, and neither of us was hurt. I am afraid I have to tell you that your wife is deceased. She did not die from the accident, or it seems as if she didn't. You need to come down to the Funeral Home to identify her body and then to the Sheriff's office to pick up her things. There was total silence on the other end of the line except for a man crying and saying Oh No, Oh No. The man regained his composure and told Clifford he would be down as soon as he could get someone to come to be with his children. That is fine, you need to go to the Funeral Home, but if you need to wait to come to our office tomorrow, that will be okay.

Janet was on her cell phone telling her parents what had happened and that it would be a while before we could get there. They understood what had happened and said that they would just put their leaving off until tomorrow morning. Two wreckers had arrived on the scene and were pulling the vehicles into town to the impound lot. The Trooper gave them a ride back to their house in New Castle so they wouldn't have to call for someone to pick them up.

They fell on the couch when they got back to their house. I better call Mom and let them know what has happened since we called them from the mountain. She dialed their number, and her mother answered on the first ring. Mom, it was Jenny's sister who was in the truck. We aren't sure what happened, but the accident didn't kill her. We are at home now. What time are you guys going to leave in the morning? We want to get out of here around eight o'clock. Can you and Cliff make it up here by then? Sure, Mom, we will be there, but not with bells on. I'll bring a box of tissues. I am happy for you and Dad, but tomorrow, I plan on doing some crying. That will make two of us, honey, maybe three; I expect your father will do some tear-shedding himself. Goodnight, honey; we will see you in the morning. Janet hung up the phone and started crying. The only thing he could do was put his arms around her and let her cry.

The alarm went off at six a.m., and Janet slid out from between the sheets, walked down the hall into the kitchen, poured the water into the coffee maker tank, and flipped the switch on. She felt a whole lot better this morning about her parent's move, she would miss them but knew they would be better off in a warmer climate. She went into the bedroom and rousted Cliff from the bed. As usual, he was standing tall and ready. Sorry bud, not this morning, get your butt out of bed. We only have an hour or so before we need to go up to my parents to tell them goodbye. She went back to the kitchen and made some oatmeal for them to eat and put some toast on to have with it. Cliff came in already dressed, but she could tell by the imprint of his member in the front of his pants that he was in dire need this morning, but he would just have to get over it for the time being. She walked over to him and reached over and rubbed his penis through his jeans, and said, big boy, later, I promise. They sat down at the kitchen table and enjoyed their breakfast together. She hadn't dressed yet, so she went to the bedroom and put on some jeans and a sweatshirt. It was now 7:30 am, and she knew her parents wanted to leave at eight o'clock, so she made him get into the car, and they headed up the mountain to the home she grew up in and would be moving back to in a few weeks.

They pulled into the driveway and could see her father closing the back of the small U-Haul that they had rented to carry what belongings they were taking with them. She got out of the car and walked over to her father, grabbed him, and gave him a bear hug and a kiss on the cheek. The three of them went into the house, where she found her mother in the kitchen, cleaning the refrigerator out. Mom, what are you doing? I will take care of all the cleaning that needs to be done. Give me a big hug and kiss, and then you and Dad get into the car and head out of here before it snows, and you can't go. Her mother threw the cleaning cloth into the kitchen sink, grabbed her daughter, hugged her, and kissed her. You two, we will expect you down to Florida for Christmas, no if, and or butts about it. Yes, Mom, we will be there before December 24th. Her parents got into their truck and headed west on Route 42. Janet could see both of them wiping away tears from their eyes, just as she was doing. Cliff wasn't wiping, but she could see the moisture in his eyes. She knew that he had grown to love her parents just as she did.

While we are here, Cliff we had better look at that refrigerator and make sure Mom took everything out that will spoil before we move in here. You're right, dear; let's go check right this moment before something spoils while we are standing here. She shook her fist at him, and they went into the house to check out things. Her mother had done her job as usual, so they did not find anything that they needed to take care of today. They went out the door and Clifford locked the door and handed the key to her. Now, Janet, we have plenty of time to finish cleaning our house and moving everything we want to keep up here, so don't get in such a whirlwind about moving. I won't, Cliff. I know we have plenty of time, but you know me, I want things done right this instant. Oh yes, I sure do know how you are; it didn't take me but about a week to steer clear of you when you got into one of your rampages. You're like a bull in a China shop when you start a project. But dear, I love you just the way you are! He leaned down and gave her a juicy, wet kiss on the mouth. I still remember the promise you made to my Johnny this morning and he is going to hold you to it when we get home. Indeed, he did; they didn't even stop in the kitchen; they went directly to the bedroom, shedding their clothes as they went down the hall. Four hours later, after they had showered, they went to the kitchen for some food. Both of them had worked up a very good appetite.

Janet fixed them a hardy meal of Beef tips and a loaded baked potato, no bread, that was too fattening or so she told him. They relaxed in front of the TV for a few hours and then went to bed early. They both knew they would have a long day tomorrow trying to finish cleaning out the house they were living in. Janet and her mother had pretty much-gleaned everything not needed or wanted from their new house.

The next morning, they slept in until about nine a.m. She fixed them some light breakfast and once it was over, she forced Cliff to begin pitching items from the basement den. She had to stay right with him and double-question him when he laid trash in the keep pile. Noon came and went, but they did not stop for a snack. She looked at her watch and saw that it was now four o'clock, well big boy, it is time to get off work for the day. I am proud of you my dear; you have done a great job today. In about two to three more we will be done and ready to move it all up on the mountain. He just smiled at her and replied, yes, dear. She smiled back and replied, dear, you are learning quickly to listen to the boss. He had taken off all this week because he knew that he would have to be around to help, or Janet would have free range to throw away whatever she didn't want to keep.

All week long, he was the endearing husband and did everything he was asked to do. He loved this woman and wanted to make her happy, but occasionally, he had to keep his happiness in tack. They worked their butts off all week, but by Friday, everything was done, and they were ready to start taking boxes of their stuff to the new house. They decided to take about four boxes to the new house each night after supper and unload the boxes in the new house, placing the items in the rooms where they belonged. This worked out to be a good plan, by the end of the first week, they had almost all of the boxes taken to the new house and unpacked and placed where the item belonged. He had made arrangements with a couple of guys around town to help him move what furniture they kept to the new house. At the end of the two weeks after her parents had left, they were ready to stay in the new house. Janet went back to the old house the following week and cleaned everything till it was spotless and shinned like stars.

She hoped the house here sold as quickly as her Richmond Condo had. She had called the local Realtor and was meeting them at the house today at two o'clock. She arrived at the old house at about 1:45 and went on in to double-check things. The Realtor rang the doorbell at two o'clock, just as she said she would. Janet let her in and began to take her through the house, pointing out any of the extras that most houses may not be equipped with. The Realtor did not show much emotion while they walked through. When they had looked at all of the house, Janet asked her, Sheila, I couldn't tell from your facial expressions if you liked the house or not.

Sheila looked her directly in the face and point blankly said: I love it, and I believe I have a buyer for you. I have been on the lookout for a house just like this one for a buyer who wants to move out of Roanoke but not into the countryside per se. That is great. We have removed everything that we want to keep. The new owners get everything that is left here; if they don't want it, they can dispose of it in whatever method they choose. Sheila Dehart told Janet that she would get in touch with her prospective buyer and let her know what he said. Sounds good to me Janet said, we will be looking forward to getting your call. She went back home to their new house and could hardly wait for Cliff to get home so she could tell him the good news.

Cliff came into the living room, and she met him to tell him what had happened with the realtor. He was pleased that they may already have a buyer, but how about the asking price?

Last night, we talked, and you said that you thought we should ask at least $178,000 for it. Sheila looked it over and said that she wanted to put an asking price of $195,000 and see what her buyer would offer. She knows we won't take less than our price, but she seems to think we can get more. We will have to wait and see what happens. She had supper ready, and all she had to do was put it on the table. He was hungry and lit into the corn on the cob like a little pig at the trough. He had eaten three ears of corn before he even started on the meatloaf and mashed potatoes.

It had been a rough day at work, and now he was stuffed with good food. He went into the living room, sat down in his recliner, switched the TV on, and was snoring within two minutes. She got a blanket, spread over him, and sat down in her chair and before she knew it, she was asleep. Cliff awoke and looked at the clock on the TV and saw that it was after one a.m., and he and Janet had been asleep in their chair ever since dinner. He gently rubbed her arm, and she awoke and smiled at him. Come on, sleepy head, let's go to bed. They both walked down the hall and didn't even take their clothes off before they slid into the bed.

It was a good thing that the new house had one bedroom downstairs; they might not have been able to climb the flight of steps to get upstairs. Clifford awoke when the alarm went off the next morning at six a.m. He went into the kitchen and poured the water into the coffee maker and turned the switch on. Janet awoke to the sound of the shower running and knew that Cliff was in it, so she quietly joined him there for a morning romp. These episodes were beginning to happen more frequently, and she didn't mind one bit. She loved this man and could not get enough of him. He toweled her down, and she put on her robe and went into the kitchen to get breakfast ready. He came into the kitchen with a smile on his face. Oh, sit down and eat your breakfast, little boy. They enjoyed their breakfast together, and Clifford headed out to the office to find out what had gone on during the night. It had been two weeks since he had given Jake the knife, and he had not heard anything from him concerning it. He did say that it was going to take a while to hear from the London company. He had also given him the pictures that he had taken from the tower and Jake had not said anything about them. Now, Clifford, be patient; Rome wasn't built in a day.

Chapter Twenty

Clifford was glad that he had kept a copy of the fingerprints that were on the knife and a picture of the knife. If the original was lost for any reason, there was a backup plan. It wouldn't be as good as the original, but it would do if it became necessary. It was quiet in the office this morning. The Deputies were out making their runs around the county checking on things. Most of the time, everything was okay, but occasionally, they would find a car that had stopped on someone, and they would put a tag on it. Vehicles had to be moved within so many days, or they would be towed by the county, and the owner would be responsible for the tow bill. Things were pretty quiet in the county, except when there was a murder. John Moore's murder was the first one the county had experienced in twenty years, and now Jill Jackson's death made the second one in two years. I sure hope this is not a pattern that will continue, he thought to himself.

It was a two-day trip for Janet's parents to get to Port St. Lucie, Florida, and they had not heard from them last night and Clifford was beginning to feel uneasy about them. He would not breathe one breath of his concern around Janet because she probably would go off the deep end, and he would not blame her. His cell phone began to ring and he glanced to see who was calling him and saw that it was Janet. Hey, what's up, he said as he answered his phone. Not much; I am at the old house, just looking over things to make sure that everything is in order. Have you heard from the Realtor this morning, not yet, but I have my hopes up. She did think the people would like our old house, I guess time will tell.

He wanted to ask if her parents had called this morning, but he dared not. He did not want her to get anxious about them. He picked up his cell phone and dialed his father-in-law's number. It began to ring. He listened to it ring ten times and then hung up. He dialed his mother-in-law's number, and he experienced the same situation. Now, he was really starting to get anxious. He thought at least one of them would have been able to pick up, and neither phone let him go to voice mail. He laid the phone down on his desk and decided he would try them later.

Deputy Smith came into Clifford's office and informed him that there had been an accident in the Red Brush section of the county. How bad is the accident, Ike? Two cars hit head-on, and there is a State Trooper and an ambulance on their way. Okay, I would think that they would have everything taken care of over there. The more he thought about it, he concluded that he should get in his car and go over there, so he checked out of the office and headed to Red Brush. It would take him around twenty minutes to get there due to the road being curvy and narrow.

When he arrived on the scene of the accident, he could see car parts strewn all over the road. He parked his cruiser and walked to where the Trooper was standing, talking with the ambulance driver. He approached them and could see a person in one of the wrecked vehicles; he could tell they did not survive the crash. Morning Trooper Jones, I see at least one fatality; how about the other vehicle? Sorry to say, there is a body in the other car also. Neither person made it through the crash. Have you identified them yet, this road is sort out of the way, and I am afraid that they may be locals. It is unusual, but both cars have out-of-state tags and I don't recognize any of the names in their wallets. Both are males, and both look to be in their early to late thirties. The man that you can see is James Zimmerman from Maryland, and the other guy is Chuck Long from West Virginia. I have called their names into the office and asked them to run the tags through the appropriate state and see if they come up with a next of kin for us to notify. This little county of yours has been really hopping this year with all kinds of strange things happening. Yes, Clifford answered and added, I sure hope it slows down. The trooper had called the Funeral Home to come and pick up the bodies and hold them until the next of kin could be notified and make the arrangements.

Clifford went back to his office and immediately called Jake Edwards and told him that James Zimmerman, from Maryland, had died in an automobile accident in Craig this morning. He had to be connected to the other two guys with the same last name and also from Maryland. Jake wasn't in his office, so Clifford left him a message about the guy. Jake called him within five minutes of him leaving the message and told him he had already put in a request with their Maryland office to find out who James Zimmerman was and if he had connections with the other two Maryland men. Jake ended the conversation abruptly and did not say anything about the knife.

Clifford had hardly hung up the phone when his cell began ringing; he glanced at it and saw that it was Janet. He reached for it and answered. Hi, Janet cut him off before he could say anything else, Mom and Dad have had an accident near Savannah, Georgia, and that is the reason we have not heard from them. Dad just called. Both of them were knocked unconscious, and he had just now awakened and was able to call. Mom is still in a comma, but they think she will be all right. Neither have any broken bones, just contusions to their heads.

A tractor-trailer came into their lane, and to avoid it, Dad went to the guardrail, and the rail flipped them. They were lucky it did not flip them in the truck's path. I need to go down there right now, if I leave now, I can get there around ten tonight. Hold on just a minute, Janet, I need to finish up here, and I will come home, and both of us will go. He hung up the phone and called Ike into his office and told him what had happened and that he was leaving and would be gone for several days. He left Ike in charge while he was gone, he trusted him to take care of business.

He rushed home, and when he entered the door, he could see Janet pacing the floor. Janet calmed down. Your Dad is okay, and your Mom is going to recover. We will leave just as soon as I change clothes and grab something to drink, so just sit down and be quiet for a few minutes while I change. She went to the couch and took her seat and he went to the bedroom to change his clothes. When he came back to the living room, he asked her if she had packed them some extra clothes since they would be gone a couple of days for sure. She was so excited, she hadn't done that, so they went into the bedroom and grabbed a few items to have to change into. Getting into his private car, they started down the road. They would go to Roanoke and get on Interstate 81, then to I-77. This interstate would lead them into North Carolina, and outside of Charlotte, they would enter South Carolina and then take the exit to I-26 and then to I-95, which would take them to Georgia. In all, about eight hours of driving, a little more time if you stopped for something to eat.

The trip so far had gone uneventful, most of the drivers were being careful and paying attention. Things were about to change. Charlotte, North Carolina, is huge, and the traffic starts to bog down fifty miles before you even get there. They were in that right at the moment, and Clifford was having to watch closely at his driving. There were as many tractor-tailers as cars, and all of them were doing the 70 mph that was posted, plus another ten. He did not like to travel more than five miles per hour above the posted speed limit, but in this traffic, if you didn't keep up, you may get run over, so Clifford was keeping it right on 80 just to keep up with the traffic and not create a problem for the other drivers who would have to go around him if he were going below that speed. It took them another hour and a half to get through Charlotte; the traffic was terrible, but they made it. They were south of Charlotte and had just crossed over to South Carolina; Clifford could see the exit to Rock Hill. Are you hungry? Yes, she answered, so he took the exit, he knew there were plenty of places to eat there.

A couple of blocks off of the exit, they were able to pull into a Ruby Tuesdays to get some supper. The restaurant did not have many cars in the lot, and when they entered, just a few people were being served. The hostess seated them and gave them menus for them to look at. They checked them out and chose the items they wanted. They chatted for a while, and Clifford glanced at his watch and could see they had been seated for twenty minutes, and the server hadn't returned.

A server was walking by their table, and he spoke to that server in a loud voice, sir, can you help me? The guy stopped and looked around at him and, with a glare, asked him what he needed. I need a server to take our orders; we have been here for over twenty minutes with no service. I don't usually service this table, but since you have been neglected, I will take your orders for you and get them in quickly. They told the guy what they had chosen, and he put it in his hand-held computer. Sir, it will take approximately twenty more minutes for the kitchen to get this out. What would you like to drink with your meal? I want regular coffee, and she would like water with a slice of lemon. He brought their drinks right away and apologized for them being overlooked. He had the food on their table before the twenty minutes was up.

They gobbled their dinners down in a hurry because they wanted to get back on the road so they would get into Savannah before it got too late. Cliff saw the server who finally waited on them and, handed him a Ten-dollar tip and thanked him for waiting on them. The GPS shows another four hours before we get to Savannah. Janet, do you think the hospital will let us in when we get there? I don't know, but I would think they would, under the conditions why we are here. They got back on I-77, and it would take them another hour or so to get to I-26, which would take them outside of Charleston, South Carolina, where they would pick up I-95. It would be straight sailing to Savannah on I-95, although the road through South Carolina on 95 can get rather bumpy with potholes.

The time was 10:10 p.m., and they were still a good hour outside of Savannah. Janet, I think you should call your father on his cell and tell him we are getting in late and that we will come to the hospital early in the morning. I think you are right; she dialed her father's number. It rang four times, and he picked it up. Dad, we are about an hour outside of Savannah. It looks like it is too late for us to come to the hospital tonight, so we will get a room and come early tomorrow to the hospital. That sounds good, honey. Get a good night's rest, and I will see you in the morning. They were almost into Savannah by this time, and Cliff was looking for a hotel off of one of the exits. He was tired of driving and ready to stop.

There was an Embassy Suites off the next exit, and Clifford took the exit and went to the hotel. They were lucky; the hotel had a vacancy, and they rented the last room they had. The room was available the next night, so Clifford booked it for two nights. They both took long hot showers and by the time they had finished, the time had already clicked over midnight, so they snuggled under the covers and fell asleep. The next morning, they awoke almost at the same minute. Janet smiled at Cliff. He was lying there on his side looking at her when she opened her eyes. He reached over and gently ran his fingers across her lips; that was all it took; she moved over to him, reached under the covers, and ran her fingers down his chest and then a little farther down. She could tell he was ready for some morning action; smiling, she gave him a sloppy, moist kiss on the lips, and he took over from there.

Once showered, they went down to the dining room and had a great breakfast. Cliff got into the car and put the address of the hospital in the GPS, it came up immediately, and it had a time of arrival of thirty minutes showing. This won't take us long, honey. He shut his door and started the engine, and they were on their way there. Janet was a little anxious as they walked down the hallway of the hospital. They had stopped at the information desk and got her mother's and father's room number. Her mother had regained consciousness, and the hospital had put both her parents in the same room. When she stepped into the room, she had to force herself from gasping. Her parents were awake, but she could see the bruises and cuts on their faces. Rushing over to their beds, she gently gave each a hug and kissed on the cheek.

Her father was very talkative, but her mother didn't say much to them for a while. Mr. Moore explained what had happened and thought that the two of them were lucky to be alive and to have no broken bones was a miracle. The hospital had told them that they could be released as soon as Janet and Cliff arrived, and they had a way of leaving with some help. They helped them get dressed and called the hotel to see if there was another room available for the night. There was, so they took her parents back to their hotel. Mr. Moore and Cliff went to the impound lot to check on the truck and small U Hall they had been pulling when the accident happened. The truck was totaled, as well as the U Hall trailer, but the trailer had stayed together, so all their belongings were intact. They went and did the paperwork at the U Hall Rental store and got another trailer to put the Moore's belongings in. Most of the day was gone by the time they had changed out the trailers with the Moore's belongings. Mrs. Moore was feeling much better by the time they returned to the hotel, so much, they went out to dinner that night at the Outback Steakhouse that was located beside the hotel. Janet and Cliff would take them on their journeys last leg, to Port St. Lucie and help them with their insurance paperwork and such.

This took Janet and Cliff two days and then they bid her parents goodbye in Florida and started home to New Castle. Janet was thrilled that her parents had come through that accident without any broken bones, just some bruises and scrapes. The bruises were almost gone by the time they had left to go home, it would take the cuts a little longer. The Moore's Condo was very nice on Hutchison Island and was right beside her Uncle and Aunt, so she was at ease leaving them and going back home.

Chapter Twenty-One

Cliff and Janet returned to New Castle the same day they had left her parent's place in Florida. They had driven straight through, and it had taken them thirteen hours. Both were dead tired when they pulled into their driveway but glad to be home. It was one o'clock in the morning, so they pulled off their clothes and slid between the sheets. They were asleep by the time their heads hit their pillows and did not wake up until the next morning. Janet got up and went to the kitchen and put the coffee on and it wasn't very many minutes before Cliff came staggering into the kitchen. He gave her a peck on the cheek, got a cup of coffee, and sat down at the table. Good morning, she said to him, and good morning to you also was his come back to her. They ate the toast and honey that she had prepared for them without saying very much to one another. What is wrong this morning, Cliff asked Janet. Oh nothing, I am just tired from all of this moving and running around. Yeah, it does take a toll on you. Maybe we can slow down a little now that we have your parents settled in Florida. I hope so, she said; you had better get dressed if you are planning on going into the office on time this morning. He got up from his chair and headed into the bedroom to dress.

A few minutes later, he returned with his uniform on, kissed her, and left for the office. She cleaned up the kitchen and made the bed before she sat down to have another cup of coffee. She poured her the coffee, and about that time, the phone rang. Picking it up, she could see it was the Realtor. Morning, Sheila spoke. I have good news for you this morning. I showed your house while you were gone, and the clients loved it. They came with an offer this morning of $187,500.00. That is exactly what I was hoping they would offer, right between what you thought and what I asked. I will call Cliff and see if he agrees and will call you back in a few minutes. She hung up the phone and immediately called Cliff on his cell phone. He answered on the first ring. What's wrong, honey? Nothing dear, the Realtor called, and the people offered us $187,500.00 for the house. Are you okay with accepting the offer? You bet I am. Just call her back and tell her to sell it to them today, and I will make myself available to sign the papers. Everything was good this morning; I just need to hold my breath for a few minutes to see if the peace will remain.

Clifford decided that he needed to call Jake Edwards and see what had happened with the knife and the fingerprint that he had found at the Tower. He dialed Jake's number at the FBI, and it started ringing, a woman answered, saying Charles Dumont's office. Clifford was silent for a minute, thinking he must have dialed the wrong number. He finally answered her with, I am sorry, I was or thought I was dialing Jake Edwards's number. Mr. Edwards has retired, and Mr. Dumont has taken over his duties. Clifford could not believe what he was hearing from this woman. I am sorry, ma'am. I am Clifford Davidson, the Sheriff of Craig County, and agent Edwards and I have been working on a murder case, and he had not mentioned to me that he was going to retire.

The lady replied, no one knew; he came in the other day and announced that he was going to retire. If that is the case, I need to make an appointment with Agent Dumont; we will want to go over some facts in the murder case that Jake and I have been working on together. Mr. Dumont has an opening tomorrow at 2:00. Can you be in Richmond by then? Richmond? Yes, Sheriff, Mr. Dumont's office is in Richmond. If that is the case, I will be there tomorrow to make the appointment. I will have to leave around eight o'clock in the morning to make the meeting, but it won't be the first time I have made an early trip to Richmond. He went home and told Janet what had happened and that he would be going to Richmond early tomorrow morning. He invited her to ride along if she would like to go visit some of her newspaper friends while he had his meeting, and she accepted his invitation. They went to bed early that night so they could get up early and leave for Richmond.

The trip went well between New Castle and Richmond and they arrived there in time to have lunch with one of their friends. Clifford left Janet at the newspaper office and he went to the FBI building for his meeting. Taking the elevator up to the sixth floor, he got off right at the door to Agent Dumont's office. He opened the door and walked into the room. The secretary greeted him, and Clifford introduced himself. Just have a seat, Sheriff, and I will tell Agent Dumont that you are here. She returned and told Clifford that Agent Dumont would see him shortly. The new agent came out and shook his hand and ushered him into his office. I know all of this is disturbing to you, but I will do my best to pick up the pieces that Jake Edwards may have left unattended. There are a couple of things that Agent Edwards was working on and had not gotten back to me with answers.

I have gone over all of his notes, especially the ones concerning the Tower Murder, but he doesn't have anything to indicate that something is outstanding to be looked into at this time. Clifford's mouth must have fallen wide open upon hearing what Agent

Dumont just said to him. Did Agent Edwards mention anything concerning a knife and a fingerprint found at the Tower, later by myself and my wife? He got out the notes and looked again, I do not see anything about a knife nor a fingerprint found after the FBI had done their investigation up at the Tower. Something isn't right here, Agent Dumont.

I gave Edwards the knife and a copy of the fingerprint that I found and could not identify through your fingerprint records. I am sorry, Sheriff, but there is no record in his notes addressing either of the items that you have just told me about. I am at a loss as to why Edwards would not have this in his notes. The last time I talked with him, he advised me that he had checked with the knife store at the Valley View Mall and they were checking with their parent store in London, England as to who may have bought the knife. The knife was engraved with the initials CCC on its handle. The store had told Edwards that a special item, such as this knife that had engraving, came directly from England and not through their store. He told me they were checking with their parent company and he would let me know what he found out. I had located a fingerprint underneath the top railing at the Tower that you guys had missed, but when I ran it, you did not have a match in your files.

I am sorry, Sheriff, I don't know what to tell you, but I can assure you that we do not have anything in our files indicating the items that you just informed me of. I have several pictures of the knife showing the initials, and I still have the print I found in my files. I can get these items to you so you can look into this further; there is definitely a problem here.

Agent Dumont agreed with Clifford and indicated he would be

eagerly awaiting the information that Clifford would be sending him. Disappointed, Clifford left the Agent's office and headed over to the newspaper office to pick up Janet. He parked the car and went into the newspaper office and up to the third floor, where he found Janet talking with three of her old work partners. They all stood up and gave him a bear hug; Janet knew he would want to hit the road, so she said goodbye to her friends, and they went to the automobile and started home to New Castle. She could not believe what he was telling her concerning Agent Edwards and the evidence that the two of them had found at the Tower. They stopped at a little place called Short Pump, right outside of Richmond, and ate some lunch. It would be several hours before they would get home.

Chapter Twenty-Two

The next morning, Clifford was out of bed bright and early, at six o'clock. When the alarm went off, he jumped out of bed and into the shower. He wanted to get this day started early. Janet awoke when he all but jumped out of bed and hit the shower. She wasn't as happy as Cliff about getting up early but felt she should be a supporting wife, so she got up and went to the kitchen to fix him some breakfast before he left for work. She had almost gotten everything on the table by the time he came into the kitchen completely dressed in his uniform. Whoa, Buckaroo, slow down and eat your breakfast before you go to work, she said. He gave her a grin, sat down, and began eating the breakfast that she had prepared. He did slow down and they chit-chatted over breakfast, but as soon as he had eaten the last bite, he gave her a peck on the cheek and ran out the door. Janet's only comment was: "Men, you can't live with them sometimes, and most of the time, you don't want to live without them."

Clifford went into his office and started digging in his top drawer looking for the pictures of the knife and the fingerprint copy. He was sure he had put them here, but he was almost through all of the papers, and he had not come up with the evidence he was looking for. Calling his secretary, hey Julie, do you know where I put the knife pictures and fingerprint from the Tower? Clifford, you know you left them on your desk and told me to put them in the folder in the file cabinet named The Tower. Now I remember, yes, you're right, Julie; how about getting the folder for me? Julie came into his office carrying the folder and placed it in front of him on his desk. Will there be anything else, Sir? She smiled as she made the statement, so he knew she was just kidding with the Sir remark. He opened the folder and sure enough, right on top were the pictures of the knife and print. He went to the fax machine, entered Agent Dumont's fax number, and pushed the send button. He had made a cover sheet before he had placed the picture copies in the machine. He stood there and watched as the machine pulled the paperwork through and sent it over the wires to the FBI headquarters in Richmond, Va. He requested that Agent Dumont let him know that he had received the information. Ten minutes later, Dumont's secretary called Clifford and advised him that she had taken it off the fax and put it on Agent Dumont's desk for his review. He thanked her for letting him know that the information had been received.

He picked up his cell phone and called Janet; he let it ring ten times before she finally picked it up. Okay, this better be good, I had to come downstairs to get my phone and then I had to search three rooms to find it. Just calm down, sweetie pie. I am calling to see if you want to go into Roanoke this afternoon. I want to go to the Valley View Mall to the knife store. I don't think Agent Edwards was telling me the truth concerning the knife and where it came from. I will be ready, what time are you picking me up? I will be there at two o'clock, you be ready to come out when I blow the horn. I may come out when you blow the horn this time, but I don't respond to horns and whistles very well. Clifford hung up the phone and went to the copier and made copies of the original pictures he had of the knife and print to take with him to the Knife Shop. Ike came into his office to talk with him for a few minutes, so he quit what he was doing and listened to what Ike had to tell him. He didn't like what he told him; Ike was going to retire the next month, and that meant he would be looking to hire a new deputy. He shook Ike's hand and wished him well. He pulled into his driveway at 2 pm on the dot, and Janet came out and slid into the passenger side seat. You had better take notice of me coming after you honked your horn; you probably will never witness it again. Clifford just shook his head and replied, you want to bet.

It took them about an hour to get to the mall and get parked. She went with Cliff to the Knife Shop and just stood there and looked at all the different knives they had on display. Clifford went and asked for the manager of the store. I am the manager the young man answered with a smile. I am the Sheriff over in Craig County, and I need some information on a knife that was found at a murder scene. Agent Edwards of the FBI told me he had talked with you about the knife, and you informed him that since it was engraved, it would have been shipped directly from England. The fact that it would be shipped from England is correct, but I do not remember talking with any gentleman concerning a knife such as the one in the picture that you have just shown me. Clifford did not know what to think now. Can you inquire and see if your London factory shipped a knife with the initials CCC engraved on the handle? Yes, I will be happy to do that for you, it will take a few days to get the information from them, so write down your telephone number where I can reach you. Clifford gave him the necessary information that he had requested and then he and Janet went back into the mall. Now what? Janet asked. Is there any store that you need to go to while we are here? I could use a look in Macy's while we are here and then why don't we go over to Longhorn's for some dinner? Sounds good to me; lead on to the promised land, dear. Janet just rolled her eyes at him, grabbed hold of his hand, and started down the steps that led to the lower level.

The next morning, Clifford went to his office early to check on what kind of paperwork had been put on his desk while he was gone. A few things had appeared, but he was able to take care of them in just a few minutes. He picked up his phone and dialed the number he had reached Agent Dumont on a few days ago. The phone rang a couple of times before a woman picked it up and answered Agent Dumont's Office, Doris speaking. This is Sheriff Clifford Davidson, I was there two days ago, and I need to speak to Agent Dumont, please. He is in a meeting at the moment. I will have him return your call upon his return from his meeting.

Thank you, that will be fine he replied. I will await his call; you can tell him it concerns the knife. Clifford hung up the phone and went to the break room to get a cup of coffee. Pouring him a cup, he went back to his office, and just as he sat down at his desk, the phone began to ring. Picking it up, he answered, Sheriff Davidson, speaking, how may I help you? This is Dumont in the Richmond FBI Office, Doris said you called about the knife in question. Yes, I went to the store at our mall that sells this type of knife and talked with the manager of the store, Mr. Hackney. He informed me that he had not spoken with anyone about a knife like the one in my picture. He did agree that it would have been shipped from London, England. That would be the only place to get an engraved knife of the quality that was in the picture. He has requested that the England factory research this knife sale and see if they can come up with an order for it and also an address and phone number, if possible, the name of the purchaser. I wish the FBI had taken the lead on the request, but I understand why you have gone with it. Please let me know what they come back with as soon as you know. I will, but there is one thing you need to do, and that is start an inquiry on your Agent Edwards. I am afraid he is up to his ears concerning the drugs and murders in Craig County. He played his part well, but things are looking bad in his direction now. I hope you guys can find where he might have gone upon his retirement. Two to One, it is someplace where he cannot be brought back to the U.S. for trial. I hope not, Dumont replied, but we will find out where he is, for sure.

Clifford started thinking about the fingerprint and the fact there was no match for it in the data bank. I just wonder if Jake Edwards's fingerprints were filed anywhere else; the print I found could match his.

Clifford quit for the day and went home to see what Janet was doing. He walked in the door and could see her standing in the kitchen at the stove, stirring something. He walked up behind her, put his arms around her waist, and kissed her on the back of the neck. Wow, what brought that on, big boy, she said with a big smile on her face. Just missed you today, my sweet, so what have you done today and what's that you are cooking? Well, I have been busy going through Mom's closet; she said she was leaving everything she didn't want right where it was. I wouldn't have believed my mother owned so many pieces of clothing. I am a much taller woman, so most of the clothing pieces are two short-waisted, and I can't wear them. The Goodwill will be happy to get them; most don't look like they were ever worn, and some even have sale tags on them from the store. I wonder if they would take them back without a sales receipt. With that, she gave out a chuckle. What is funny, my dad took every stitch he owned; it looks like you don't get anything from his closet. Cliff smiled and said, Honey, I already have too many clothes as it is. She was boiling icing to put on her German Chocolate Cake that she had already taken out of the oven. She could see the gleam in his eyes when he saw what she was making. Looks like I will have to put my belt in another hole after I eat most of that cake. What's for supper? He asked. We are having fried chicken, mashed potatoes, green beans, and hard-tack biscuits. Honey, are you trying to make me look like Santa Claus? They sat down at the table, and Cliff over-ate as usual; he told himself he had to slow down on the food intake. He helped her clean up the dishes, and then they went into the living room to watch some TV before bedtime. Cliff filled her in on all of the day's work concerning the Tower murder.

They went to the bedroom around ten o'clock, and by then, he had digested most of his supper, so he got into the mood when he saw her undress and go to the shower. She knew what would happen when she got naked to go to the shower, and she was fine with it. He immediately got excited, peeled his clothes off, and stepped into the shower with her. She was always amazed at how he was always up for the occasion without her helping him out. If the truth be known, she would like to help him to get up and ready for action. The alarm started ringing way before she was ready to get up, but like a good little wife, she arose and went to the kitchen, poured the water into the coffee maker tank, switched the warmer on, and closed the lid to start the process. She didn't want to do bacon and eggs; this morning, he would have to be okay with toast with honey on it. Clifford came creeping wearing nothing but a towel., not now Cliff.

It is too early for a romp. Now honey, I am not here wearing this towel trying for a romp, all my clean underwear is in the laundry room. Likely story she spit out. Now get in there, and put some clothes on. He went into the laundry room, pulled a pair of jockeys out of the dryer, and put them on. The jockeys didn't hide his huge bulge in the front, but Janet still was not affected, she wasn't in the mood this morning. He was like a little boy who had been scolded by his mama.

When he didn't get his way, his bottom lip tended to stick out in a pout. She smacked him on the butt as he passed by her on the way to the bedroom. In a few minutes, he came back fully dressed in his uniform, kissed her, and went out the door to work.

He went into his office, sat down at his desk, and started looking at the sticky notes that Julie had placed on his desk. Most of them had already been taken care of by one of the deputies. One was from the manager of the Knife Store at the mall. The knife was ordered by Jill Jackson and shipped to 333 Oakland Blvd, Roanoke, Va. He called Agent Dumont and was surprised that he picked up the phone and did not have the secretary answer it. This is Davidson, over in Craig County, I heard back from the Knife Store. The knife was bought by the murdered woman, Jill Jackson, but was shipped to 333 Oakland Blvd, Roanoke, Va. We do not have an address for Miss Jackson for this address. Do you have a home address for Jake Edwards? Also, do you have Edwards's fingerprints on file? If not, can you get them? I have a gut feeling that he lives or did live at the 333 Oakland Blvd address, and the fingerprint I found was his. That is probably why he did not follow up on the knife and has retired and most likely has left the country. Let me dig into these two questions and I will get back to you as soon as I can find out something.

Clifford was so tired of the FBI stumping their toes on the evidence and then not following up in a timely manner. He understood that, as a little Sheriff, he was at their mercy, and quite frankly, he was just about fed up with law enforcement duties being done in this manner.

Agent Dumont called him within an hour of his call, Clifford, the address of 333 Oakland Blvd is indeed Jake Edwards. We cannot tie him together with Jill Jackson, but we will continue to search. Looking at his employment records, we did not come up with his fingerprints, they should have been there and also in our data bank. His prints have been removed from both locations, but we have one more option to get his prints. Most people don't know, but we keep a second file of all prints in Washington, D.C. I have faxed the print you gave me and am having them run it against the file they have there. It is a large file, so it is going to take us until tomorrow to hear from that office. Agent Dumont would let him know tomorrow what the outcome is from the print run. Dumont told him as of yet, they had not found out where Jake Edwards had gone. He had to take a plane, but he had not used his real name and had secured a false passport to match the new name. Clifford could not believe the FBI could not run down one guy's location, again Cliff could hear, calm down Cliff, Rome wasn't built in a day. Now, who said that to me, he wondered, oh yes, it was the man they were looking for, Jake Edwards.

Clifford went home to find Janet was not there. He went through the house, and she just wasn't there. Her car was in the driveway, so he didn't think she had gone too far. He went out back and down to the barn, but she wasn't there either.

Going back into the house, he began to call out her name, but he did not get a response. Moving on to the upstairs, he started calling out her name again. Finally, he could hear a muffled voice saying, I'm up here. Where is up here? He thought as he went from room to room. Suddenly, one of the hallway doors came open and smacked him upside the head. He staggered backward a little from the blow of the door. Oh honey, I'm sorry; I did not know you were near the door. I had left it open, but it had closed itself. I have been up in the attic looking at what my parents left up there. They headed back downstairs and into the kitchen to have some supper. She had prepared cold cuts for dinner, and all she had to do was get them out of the refrigerator. She had everything out on the table within a couple of minutes. They ate their supper while Cliff filled her in on the details of the day's events. She thought like him; she just couldn't imagine the FBI being so slow on the uptake of the things in the case.

Chapter Twenty-Three

Her mother had called today, and all was going well in Florida; her parents had been out of the Condo several times to the beach. All they had to do was walk out the back door of the Condo, and they were on the beach. Her Uncle and Aunt had looked after them until their accident wounds had healed. Both of them were glad they had made the move and hoped Cliff and her, would be down for Christmas. Cliff and Janet were tired from their day's work, so they called it an early night and went to bed. Most of the time, when they called it an early night, they didn't go to sleep for an hour or so, but tonight, they both were pooped and fell asleep as soon as their heads hit their pillows.

Cliff awoke first and went to the kitchen to start the coffee brewer. He was naked as a newborn baby, but he didn't care; he was comfortable walking around in his skin. He heard Janet coming across the hallway to the kitchen, so he threw one leg over the chair arm and let everything hang free. He was the first thing she saw when she entered the kitchen. She pretended not to notice and went to the coffee maker, poured her a cup of coffee, and sat down at the table. He got up and poured him a cup of coffee, at which time Janet exclaimed, you better not spill that coffee on that member. If you do, there won't be any romping going on for a while around here.

Cliff just shook his head and went back to their bedroom and got dressed. Upon returning to the kitchen, he saw that Janet had fixed him some scrambled eggs and sausage cakes. Thanks, hon. I appreciate you fixing me food so I can start my day on a full stomach. She just said, you're welcome. Now go to work and get out of my hair. He kissed her and went out the door and onto his office.

It had been a couple of days since he had heard from Agent Dumont, but he guessed it might take a while for him to get the information as to Edward's whereabouts.

Looking at his desk, he could see a note for him to call Dumont when he came into the office. He dialed Dumont's number, and he answered immediately with Hello, Clifford. Morning Agent Dumont, I just got in and received your message to call you ASAP. Yes, I have some information, but not everything. The fingerprint that you sent me did not get a match from our Washington office either. However, we have information that Edwards is vacationing in his North Carolina vacation house on the Outer Banks of North Carolina. We are sending agents to pick him up for questioning. We still can't tie him together with Jill Jackson, but we are still looking. The day just seemed to move slower and slower with each hour that passed. It was time to go home, and Clifford had gotten up from his desk to leave when his phone rang. Hey Clifford, this is Dumont. Our guys picked Edwards up for questioning this afternoon.

He was totally surprised at being a suspect in all of this. Did he admit to knowing Jill Jackson? Yes, he did; he had been dating her until he found out what type of woman she was and had broken it off at least six months ago. He did not know anything about the knife and her. He figures she must have known when it was to be delivered and was there to pick it up when it came. I guess all of what you have told me is possible, but I have my doubts. If we just could find out whose print I found at the Tower and was on the knife also. So far, the only thing we have on Edwards is that he knew the murdered woman. How about him telling me he had checked with the knife store and the manager denying he had talked with him at all? We found out what happened there also. There are two managers, one for the daytime and one for the night. You talked with the daytime manager, we talked with the nighttime, and he verified that he had talked with Agent Edwards and had been waiting on the England office to get back. Dumont could hear the disappointment in Clifford's voice and chimed in Sheriff, Rome wasn't built in a day. Give us a little more time, and we will get the varmint responsible for this mess in your county.

Clifford started going over in his mind each piece of the puzzle of this case, one piece at a time. He was positive that the drug cartel was behind it all, but there had to be someone in Craig County who was tied into the cartel and was responsible for Jackson's death. No matter how many times he turned the facts over in his mind, he still could not come up with anything new. He finally went home and told Janet what had happened. She was like him. She thought Edwards was the guilty party. Is the FBI sure that the store manager is on the up and up with his alibi for Edwards? I don't know, but I will ask Dumont if they have checked the manager out. They need to look and see if he has put a large sum of money in his account lately, but I still feel that we are missing something or someone here in Craig County. Clifford started going over his employees and tried to see who they really were. Had they been born and raised in this county? Did any of them seem to have too much money? How close to the case did they make themselves? He concluded that only one employee matched several of those items. That was Jay Givens; he was born here and had been in the Sheriff's office a lot of years and could have covered up a lot of dirt in the past twenty years. He would have Agent Dumont run a financial report on Jay and see if anything turned up.

Cliff went home and tossed and turned. He hoped that Jay would not be involved, but the more he thought about it, he was beginning to think he just might be the one missing link. He ate his breakfast and went out of the house and to work. He called Agent Dumont as soon as he got to his desk. Hey, this is Clifford. I need a favor from you. Could you run a financial report on my Deputy Jay Jones? I have been going over and over in my mind to see if I thought there could be anyone in my office who could be involved with the drug cartel, and the only person who could be would be Jay. I hate to think this of him, but he has been with the office for over twenty years and would have the power to hide the dirt on a lot of people over the years. I will see what I can find out and let you know.

Dumont called within two hours with the dope on Jay Jones. He was raised here, but he was not born in Craig County. But was adopted by the Joneses when he was three years old. Guess what? Jill Jackson is his sister; they were separated when he was adopted. Jay has been depositing around three thousand dollars a month for the last five years. Just enough to stay under the IRS radar but to build quite a nest egg. His sister had also been making monthly deposits of $5,000.00 each month. We had seen the money in her account when she was murdered but could not find out where it was coming from. Is Deputy Jones in the office today? I think so, but I will have to check; hold on. Hey Julie, is Jay at work today? No, he isn't, but he should have been, and he has not called in telling us why not. Dumont, I think things are breaking here. Jay Jones is not here and hasn't called in. I have sent a deputy out to his house to see if he is there.

Ike called back from the Jones house. He is not here, and his cruiser is gone. Okay, Ike, thanks. Clifford put an all-points bulletin out for Jones's arrest for the murder of Jill Jackson. One hour had passed before Clifford got a phone call from the man who lived halfway up Potts Mountain. He wanted to report a County Cruiser had gone by his house going up the mountain at a high rate of speed and did not have any lights blinking. With the sounds that it made, he thought it had gone down the Logging Road at the top.

Clifford got Ike, and they headed up Potts Mountain; Clifford was headed to the Tower, if his gut was right, they would be finding Jay Jones swinging by the neck from the Tower, like his sister. They pulled up at the base of the Tower, and sure enough, they could see a body hanging from the rails of the Tower. They took their time getting up to the body. Both of them stopped twice to catch their breath. Upon arriving at the top, they pulled the body up to the landing, and at that point, they could tell that Jones was dead. He called the FBI, and they were there in an hour. In Jay's pocket, they found a confession letter stating that he had killed his sister because he felt that she would snitch on him if she was caught, and he felt he couldn't let that happen. He knew it was just a matter of time until Clifford would uncover the truth about him, his sister, and the drug cartel money. He had done what he had to do to keep from going to jail. He would not be Bubba's boy under any circumstances whatsoever. He decided since he had hung his sister, it was fitting for him to die in the same manner. He had driven to the Tower, climbed up on the railing, put the rope around his neck, and then put the cuffs on his wrists and took a dive off the railing. He signed the note Charles C. Crawford. Hence, the initials on the knife are CCC.

Agent Dumont came to Sheriff Davidson's office the next day and brought retired Agent Edwards with him. Clifford apologized to Edwards for thinking he might be involved. Hey Cliff, I thought you could be involved in John Moore's death. I guess that makes us even. Clifford went home that evening a very happy Sheriff. It felt like a ton of weight had been lifted from his shoulders. He told Janet how he felt and that a huge weight had been lifted from his thoughts.

Cliff, honey, I am so glad you feel this way because I have something to tell you. You might want to sit down for this one! I hope you will be happy about what I am about to tell you. It is a little sooner than you wanted, but my sweet. You are going to be a Daddy in Six Months!

The End

Look for my next book, The Pond, this will be coming out in a month or two.